Say Who You Are

by Keith Waterhouse and Willis Hall

WWW.SAMUELFRENCH.CO.UK
WWW.SAMUELFRENCH.COM

ISBN 978-0-573-01952-4

www.samuelfrench.co.uk
www.samuelfrench.com

For Amateur Production Enquiries

United Kingdom and World
excluding North America
plays@SamuelFrench-London.co.uk
020 7255 4302/01

Each title is subject to availability from Samuel French, depending upon country of performance.

SAY WHO YOU ARE

This play was first presented by Bridge Productions Limited at the Yvonne Arnaud Theatre, Guildford, on 3rd August 1965, and subsequently at Her Majesty's Theatre, London, with the following cast:

DAVID LORD	*Ian Carmichael*
SARAH LORD	*Jan Holden*
VALERIE PITMAN	*Dilys Laye*
STUART WHEELER	*Patrick Cargill*

Directed by SHIRLEY BUTLER

Setting by J. HUTCHINSON SCOTT

The play takes place in the top floor living-room of David and Sarah Lord's flat in Kensington, outside "The Hussar"—the pub round the corner—and places between.

ACT ONE	*About seven o'clock on a Friday evening*
ACT TWO	*Thirty minutes later*

No character in this play is intended to portray any specific person alive or dead.

The running time of this play, excluding the interval, is approximately two hours.

By the same authors

ALL THINGS BRIGHT AND BEAUTIFUL
BILLY LIAR
CELEBRATION
COME LAUGHING HOME
ENGLAND, OUR ENGLAND
THE SPONGE ROOM and SQUAT BETTY

By Willis Hall

A GLIMPSE OF THE SEA
THE LONG AND THE SHORT AND THE TALL

INTRODUCTION

Say Who You Are has brought the 'drawing-room comedy' up to date and given it the bite of 1965. In previous comedies of this type, playwrights have always managed to skirt over any real comment about the life of the day. In *Say Who You Are*, Keith Waterhouse and Willis Hall have extended the subject range considerably and touch areas which were thought taboo. For example, though the man in a comedy might like to have an extra-marital affair, the affair never left the realm of imagination. Characters rarely had strong views on behaviour or expressed attitudes contrary to the *mores* of the day. And certainly the play always had a happy ending, where all the strings were tied up neatly in an acceptable bundle to take home by an audience who, though titillated, were not offended in any way. In this play the authors cross the boundaries and leave the audience completely in the air as to the outcome at the curtain, but at the same time never abandon the realm of comedy. They manage this by a fine line: by making honest statements about certain subjects but never exploring them in depth.

Say Who You Are is a direct descendant of the 'comedy of manners'. In all high comedy, as opposed to revue or earthy comedy, the actors must not stress ponderously what is being said as the play's theme, but must keep the surface bubbling. Lightness and pace are essential to light comedy.

This should not confuse the actors as to the reality of their characters. The worst crime in comedy acting is the phoney 'funny business' and 'mugging', which too often is substituted for the creation of real people in a real situation, reacting to it and each other in a natural way. This often happens because the script is weak and unfunny; the actors can, however, have complete faith in this play. This natural manner will, of course, become extended and heightened at the climax of a scene or towards a curtain. The humour derives from the individual in a particular situation, his inability to comprehend what's happening, or his unawareness of his involvement, as, for example, in the long scene between DAVID and SARAH in Act I. As in all good Keystone Cops films, the tempo accelerates; situation overlaps situation and characters all meet together or miss each other. The director might well keep this image in the back of his mind when working on this play.

The first scene should start off at a naturalistic rhythm, as there is a lot of plot to establish and characters to introduce. This is very complicated for an audience to follow, particularly as much physical action goes on at the same time as important words are spoken. The first three scenes will be the most difficult, but after that the complications carry the play through to the final scene. This is purely a problem of timing, but the action, whether verbal or physical, must never drop for a moment. And yet never be forced.

A great deal depends on the credibility of the characters. An obvious pitfall would be to play them on a surface, brittle level, what I call bad West End-type acting. But a large proportion of the comedy would be lost this way. If the actor goes beneath the surface of the lines during rehearsals, he will find the characters exist in the round, and the different attitudes of one to each other, the mistaken identities, all add to the delight of the playing as well as to the enjoyment of the audience.

The most tricky character is VALERIE, as her attitudes towards life are quite contrary to the accepted feminine views. It is essential that the actress who plays VALERIE likes her; otherwise the part will be insurmountable and the actress will transmit her antipathy to the audience, which would throw the entire balance of the play. She must be warm and likeable, we must believe that she really loves STUART, otherwise she could become hard and nasty. The key to her character is the scene with SARAH and the scene in the second act with STUART. She's a very determined girl, the end product of the twentieth century suffragette.

DAVID is the man who tries hard at everything and never succeeds, though he would never understand why. He is quite capable of having an innocent affair with a young girl and never questioning the situation. He always seems to be caught unawares, his mind not able to keep up with events, baffled by what is happening to him, and therefore completely sympathetic to an audience.

SARAH could easily become harsh and nagging, unless played lightly and with her own sense of fun. Particularly in the scenes with DAVID, the actress should stress exasperation rather than brutal anger, and always remember that basically she loves her husband. Any manner of behaviour is acceptable if there is love behind it and enjoyment and gaiety; if it becomes harsh, the sense of comedy is lost and the audience begins to take the bickering too seriously. It is essential to all comedy that the characters remain likeable, and the actors enjoy playing them.

STUART could have the same difficulty as VALERIE, as a man who has walked out on his wife for no apparent reason is hardly sympathetic. But the actor can make the character likeable by playing up STUART's misguided superiority in the first scene with VALERIE and his tremendous desire to be accepted as a sophisticated Londoner in the pub scene with DAVID in Act I.

The staging of this play can present headaches to the director and actors, as the necessity of three distinct acting areas leaves very little space for each. The LORDS' flat is obviously the most important area, with the pub bench a close second and the telephone box very much in evidence. Lighting, while stressing the various areas, should not go up and down noticeably, as this could become very distracting.

SHIRLEY BUTLER

N.B. Interleaved producers' copies of this play are available, price 10s. 6d. (postage 8d. extra) *direct from the publishers only.*

ACT I

The set is a composite one, consisting of the following areas:
The living-room of DAVID *and* SARAH LORD*'s upstairs flat in a modern block in Kensington. One door leads into the hall and one into the bedroom.*
The lobby, lift and foot of staircase of the block of flats.
The entrance and frontage of 'The Hussar', a pub round the corner from the flats. There is a bench outside and the exterior is lit with fairy lights. It is the kind of pub where people wander out into the street with their drinks.
There is an S.T.D. telephone box outside 'The Hussar'.

About seven o'clock on a Friday evening. DAVID LORD, *almost ready to go out, stands with one foot on a chair, dusting his shoes with a Kleenex.*

DAVID (*after a little thought*) *Playboy of the Western World*—that was a good play.
(SARAH *comes in from the bedroom carrying her coat.*)
SARAH All right—name me another.
DAVID How many do you want me to name?
SARAH *Playboy of the Western World*—we saw that three years ago. Name me another.
DAVID *I* don't know. (*Thinking.*) *Hedda Gabler.*
SARAH We didn't see *Hedda Gabler.* (*Icily.*) Or at least *I* didn't see Hedda Gabler.
DAVID (*in slight confusion*) So we didn't. (*Over-explaining.*) No, we were going to go, if you remember. We had the seats.
SARAH (*enjoying his floundering*) Yes, I remember having the seats.
DAVID And then, if you recall, that charter flight fellow came

up—from Birmingham. And I was stuck with him. For the evening. Wasn't I?

(SARAH *chooses to ignore this completely. She picks up a paper and reads from the entertainments column.*)

SARAH The National Theatre.

(DAVID *grimaces.*)

The Stratford Company—*Othello.*

DAVID You're getting at me, aren't you?

SARAH I'm not getting at you at all. I'm just making suggestions. What about the Globe—The Polish State Theatre?

DAVID You realise it's in a foreign language?

SARAH So?

DAVID Well, if you want to see something foreign, why don't we go to the pictures? At least we'd get sub-titles.

SARAH (*exasperated*) All right, we'll go to the pictures. So long as we go somewhere.

DAVID Keep your wool on. (*Pause.*) What's on?

SARAH (*throwing the paper down in disgust*) I don't know what's on but at least let's get out of this flaming flat and stop arguing and see something.

DAVID (*also getting bad-tempered*) I'm ready!

SARAH Good!

(*During the above* STUART WHEELER *has entered, gone into the telephone box and dialled a number. The telephone in the living-room rings and* DAVID *picks it up.*)

DAVID (*sharply*) David Lord speaking.

(STUART *replaces the telephone immediately and walks into 'The Hussar'.* DAVID *slams the telephone down. His gust of bad temper is over immediately.*)

Well, what are we going to see?

SARAH Who was it?

DAVID I don't know. Wrong number. What are we going to see?

SARAH Did you always have this argument with her?

DAVID (*innocently*) Who?

SARAH Maxine, or whatever her name was. Was that one of the things you had in common?

DAVID Here we go again.

SARAH A good snog in the back stalls, bang-bang, gallop, gallop, Geronimo——

DAVID Actually there have been some very good Westerns.

SARAH Didn't she have a thought in her head at all, apart from——?

DAVID *Shane*, for example. That was a very good film.

SARAH (*viciously picking up her bag and gloves*) Yes, we know. And *Playboy of the Western World* was a very good play. And that was the last time we saw anything that would have taxed the imagination of a six-year-old, backward, mental defective!

DAVID Ask anybody. The Western is cinema in its purest form. It's pure cinema. *Shane. Stagecoach.* Right versus Wrong. Black versus White. With the great advantage that it's not in Polish.

(*They have reached the door on their way out.* VALERIE PITMAN *has entered the telephone box and dialled a number. The telephone rings in the living-room.*)

SARAH (*hastily*) I'll get it—you get a taxi.

(DAVID *goes out.* SARAH *picks up the telephone.*)

Hello?

(*We hear the rapid pips of the S.T.D. phone system before* VALERIE *puts a coin in the box.*)

VALERIE Sarah? It's Valerie.

SARAH David's gone. I'm just leaving. This minute.

(*They put down their telephones simultaneously, both pausing a moment with their hands on the receiver rest, both wearing the same expression of feminine secrecy.* DAVID *enters the lobby from the stairs.* SARAH *again collects her bag and gloves and goes out.* VALERIE *leaves the telephone box and enters the lobby. She presses the button for the lift, which does not come.* DAVID *eyes her up and down speculatively. Embarrassed by the appreciative glances of a stranger, she decides to take the stairs. As* VALERIE *goes up the stairs we see the light of the descending lift.* SARAH *steps out of the lift.*)

Have you got one?

DAVID What?

SARAH Why is it that every time you set off for a taxi I find you in the lobby saying 'What'?

DAVID Because every time I get a taxi I have to wait twenty

minutes for you to come down two flights of stairs.

SARAH Naturally you wait twenty minutes. I quite specifically take twenty minutes. I allow you twenty minutes to stand around here saying 'what'.

(Bickering, they move out of the lobby. STUART *has entered the telephone box and dialled a number. The telephone in the living-room is ringing as* VALERIE *enters. She picks it up.)*

VALERIE Hello?

(We hear the S.T.D. and STUART *puts a coin in the box.)*

STUART Valerie?

VALERIE Yes, it's all right. He's gone.

STUART Can I come up?

VALERIE *(softly)* Yes.

(They both put down their receivers. STUART *leaves the telephone box, enters the lobby and goes up in the lift.* VALERIE *rapidly takes off her coat and flings it into the bedroom. She opens her handbag and takes out a framed photograph of herself. She puts it on a small table where there is already a framed photograph of* SARAH. *She picks up the photograph of* SARAH *and puts it in her handbag. The doorbell rings.)*

VALERIE It's open!

(She moves into the bedroom as STUART *enters. She calls to him.)*

Shan't be a minute.

*(*STUART *pads self-consciously about the room. He picks up some letters and holds them up to the light in the vague hope of reading their contents, puts them down again and lets his eye fall fondly on the photograph of* VALERIE. *She comes in from the bedroom now wearing a pretty housecoat and looking completely the mistress of the house. She crosses to him and they kiss.)*

You're late.

STUART No. I was here on the dot. I rang ten minutes ago.

VALERIE Oh? Did I answer?

STUART *(with a curious look at her)* No, your husband did.

VALERIE Oh, yes! Of course! I mean I knew the phone had rung, but I couldn't remember—— Did you speak to him?

STUART Of course not. I put the phone down. As I always do.

VALERIE Of course. That was you, was it?

STUART It sounded like one of his off-days—again.

VALERIE Did it?

STUART Well, didn't it?

VALERIE Oh! (*In a martyred voice*) Oh, he's always like that.

STUART What time's he coming back?

VALERIE I don't know and I don't care!

STUART (*taking her in his arms*) Darling! (*After a decent pause.*) Ten? Eleven?

VALERIE He can stay out all night if he feels like it!

STUART If only he would.

VALERIE Forget him. We've got three hours.

(STUART *glances surreptitiously at his watch as he sits down.* VALERIE *crosses to pour drinks. She is quite familiar with the layout of the flat and always goes to the right place for the right things.*)

STUART (*romantically*) Three hours! It'll seem like three minutes! (*With another anxious glance at his watch.*) We'd better make it two and a half to be on the safe side.

VALERIE Leave the safety margin to me. Scotch, darling?

STUART Long one.

VALERIE (*holding up an empty bottle*) I'm afraid the lord and master's beaten you to it. Gin?

(STUART *rises and walks to the drinks table.*)

STUART Oh—anything. Ah! Scotch! (*He picks up a full bottle.*)

VALERIE Ah—yes. But the thing is, I don't think he'd want me to open it.

STUART For God's sake, Valerie, we know he's tight but surely he doesn't begrudge you a glass of whisky.

VALERIE No. But the whole point is, I don't drink whisky.

STUART You always drink whisky. I've never known you drink anything but whisky.

VALERIE With you, yes. But not with him. It's different with you —somehow. (*Inspired.*) It's—it's our drink.

STUART (*smiling*) We can't always have what we want, can we?

VALERIE Gin and tonic?

STUART Lovely. A long one.

(*He sits.* VALERIE *pours the drinks.*)

VALERIE I shall have to break you of this passion for long drinks.

STUART Why?

VALERIE (*delicately*) Well, it—it eats into the evening, doesn't it?

STUART It doesn't have to.

(VALERIE *has crossed, handed him his drink and now sits beside him.*)

VALERIE Not necessarily.

STUART After all, we're in control.

VALERIE (*close to him*) Are we?

(*They sit contentedly, thinking their lascivious thoughts and sipping their drinks. His face clouds over.*)

STUART Is this what you drink with him?

VALERIE (*off-guard*) Who?

STUART Is this "our drink"? With David?

VALERIE (*resignedly*) Here we go again.

STUART I'm just asking, that's all. I'm interested. After all, he's your husband. Why shouldn't you? It's not my business. I'm just curious. Do you sit here—with him—night after night—drinking gin?

VALERIE Except on Fridays.

STUART Yes, we quite understand about Fridays. We know all about our little three hour ration, thank you very much. I'm asking about the other nights. What do you do? What do you get up to?

VALERIE We don't "get up" to anything. We've been married for seven years.

STUART Valerie, you are a passionate woman——

VALERIE Not with everybody!

STUART So you say——

VALERIE Stuart, I'm passionately in love with you!

STUART All right. Granted. I believe you. The fact still remains that you are a passionate woman.

VALERIE Don't be disgusting.

STUART On your own admission, darling. You sit here—night after night——

VALERIE Except Fridays.

STUART Fridays excepted. Guzzling gin. Darling, I know you. I know what you're like. You're warm, generous—you have a generous nature. You can't tell me that with six gins

THE HUSSAR
TELEPHONE
DOUBLE DIAMOND
THE HUSSAR

inside you, you're not going to be away—(*Indicating the bedroom.*)—through there, bouncing about on the bed-springs.

VALERIE Get out!

STUART (*hastily*) Or perhaps you don't. I don't know. I don't want to know. I'm not blaming you. It's nothing to do with me. It's entirely your own life.

VALERIE Exactly.

STUART Exactly. (*A pause.*) Since that's the way you want it. (*A pause.*) Isn't it?

VALERIE Yes.

STUART Very well then. We know where we are. Three hours every Friday. Thus far and no further. (*He tosses down his drink and bangs down the glass.*) All right. I'm ready.

VALERIE (*reproachfully*) Stuart!

STUART (*mock-innocently*) What? It's what you want, isn't it?

VALERIE No, it isn't! It's nothing of the kind!

STUART Patently it is. What else do you want from me? What else am I allowed to give? Nothing. We never go out together, we never eat together. We never talk. We've no communication. We do not communicate.

VALERIE All right, we'll communicate.

STUART Thank you.

(*They settle down for communication.*)

VALERIE What would you like to communicate about first?

(*Pause.*)

STUART The Arts. We could discuss the Arts.

VALERIE I've no wish to discuss the Arts.

STUART Really? That's curious. You complain bitterly about the lack of cultural rapport between you and him. The intellectual element that's missing in your life. Come on, we'll talk about the Arts. Pick an Art.

VALERIE (*sarcastic*) Basket-weaving.

STUART (*ignoring this*) The Art of Literature. The Art of Painting.

VALERIE Stuart, let's be serious.

STUART The Flemish School. The Post-Impressionists.

VALERIE Stuart, I'm trying to talk to you.

STUART (*ponderously*) How does your moronic husband assess the influence of Bruegel the Elder on Bruegel the Younger? Or does he——

VALERIE For God's sake shut up about the rotten arts!

STUART (*also shouting*) Why? Isn't it "our topic"? Is it *his*? Like it's his flat and his whisky and his bloody gin?

VALERIE I don't want to talk about the arts to anybody.

STUART You mean with me.

VALERIE I mean with anybody.

STUART On your own admission you are stuck with a man whose last cultural expedition was three years ago. *Playboy of the Western World*. What are you saving yourself for? A revival?

VALERIE (*reasoning*) Darling, please listen. We have three hours a week together. It could be a long time—if we used it properly.

STUART Don't be disgusting.

VALERIE We love each other. We want each other. It used to be marvellous. You didn't stand there arguing three months ago. You used to stride in and—well, we had a sense of priorities. And it was marvellous. And I want it to be like that again. And you can take the Arts—and Literature—and Bruegel the Elder—and Bruegel the Younger—and *Playboy of the Western World*—all I want is you!

STUART But Valerie, we are living in a civilised world. What distinguishes man from the animals? Man is a thinking animal, a gregarious animal, a political animal.

VALERIE Then for God's sake go away and vote for somebody.

(*She turns away.* STUART *toys unhappily with his drink. Eventually*:)

STUART I think the Tories should romp it next time.

VALERIE Oh, shut up!

STUART It was meant to be a joke.

VALERIE It was in bad taste.

STUART I didn't think so.

VALERIE Stop bickering! We haven't got time for arguments and quarrels and rows. It's all we ever do these days. We might as well be married.

STUART (*sadly*) We are married.

VALERIE Yes, but not to each other. And we won't go into that again, thank you very much.

STUART Where is he tonight, anyway?

VALERIE (*off-guard*) Who?

STUART David. The wandering minstrel. The thing of shreds and patches. Business still going down the drain, I hope.

VALERIE There's no need to be cruel.

STUART Well, I mean—I don't profess to be a tycoon myself, but at least I've got *some* nous. I've got something ticking away up here. I don't set myself up as a travel agent in a small way, three doors from Cook's.

VALERIE It was the only site he could get at the rent he could pay.

STUART Oh, I was forgetting. He wouldn't have had funds available after that foray into the wine business.

VALERIE Anybody can have bad luck.

STUART Quite. I'm sure there are many people who'd've loved Portuguese Champagne. Pity the French Government took such a high-handed attitude.

VALERIE At least he tries to be a success.

STUART Suggesting what? That I don't?

VALERIE Why do you have to take offence at everything? You're as bad as he is.

STUART Go on, lump us together.

VALERIE Why not? In some ways you're very much alike.

STUART (*incredulously*) What!

VALERIE Well, you are!

STUART Me? Like him? Be fair! Drifting from one profession to a—— Well, I have tried my hand at one or two things. But, I'll tell you this, I do at least seize life with both hands. I do grab at opportunities. I have got some guts. Where am I tonight? Out with my mistress. Where's he?

VALERIE Out with his mistress.

STUART Yes, well—— Still Maxine?

VALERIE Who else?

STUART And where does he claim to be?

VALERIE He's supposed to be entertaining a client. Some charter flight man from Birmingham.

STUART Now, there's an example of the man's stupidity. A story that could easily be checked. What man from Birmingham? Where's he staying? Which hotel? Which restaurant? Why doesn't he bring him home for dinner? Why every Friday? The man's got no imagination.

VALERIE Where are you supposed to be?

STUART At the pictures.

VALERIE Hah.

STUART Yes, it sounds simple. It happens that I like the pictures and she doesn't. But the point is—the subtlety of the whole thing is, that there is no alibi to be checked. No third party. No involved story. Short of going down the aisles with a torch, there's nothing she can do to prove otherwise.

VALERIE What film are you sitting through tonight?

STUART I hadn't thought. I don't know, a Western probably.

VALERIE (*smiling*) So much for Bruegel the Elder.

STUART Not at all. Actually there have been some very good Westerns.

VALERIE We've only got two hours left, Stuart.

STUART *Shane*, for example.

VALERIE Take me to bed, Stuart.

STUART *Stagecoach*. That was a good film.

VALERIE Please.

STUART (*taking a deep, enthusiastic breath*) Actually, the whole point about Westerns is that you've got cinema in its absolutely purest—— (*He has tailed off as the prospect of* VALERIE *in bed suddenly hits him.*) Come on!

(STUART *takes* VALERIE*'s elbow and they march rapidly into the bedroom. As the door closes behind them so* DAVID *and* SARAH *march past "The Hussar" and into the lobby —or rather* DAVID *is marching and* SARAH *is trotting imploringly behind him.*)

SARAH David, please!

DAVID (*implacably*) Sorry.

SARAH Please, David!

DAVID (*stops and turns to her*) Well?

SARAH I'm sorry.

DAVID It's gone beyond that stage. (*He marches up to the lift and presses the button.*)

SARAH David, I wasn't picking on you!

DAVID Huh!

SARAH I thought we were having an interesting discussion, that's all.

DAVID There was a woman in the queue laughing at me.

SARAH She wasn't laughing at you, she was——

DAVID She was laughing at me. I made the quite reasonable point that, were I to go into the export trade, I would address my foreign customer in his own language. Was it too much to ask, I thought it a valid point, that the Italian film moguls should offer the same courtesy. And you said——

SARAH I know what I said, love. All I said, in a laughing kind of way, was that you were pig-ignorant.

DAVID And that woman burst out laughing.

SARAH She wasn't laughing at you! If she was laughing at all, she was laughing at me. Perhaps she thought I was a snob.

DAVID Good. You are. Anyway, she wasn't laughing at you, she was laughing at me. Well, I'm not a busker, Sarah. It's not my role in life to entertain the queues outside the Paris-Pullman. (*Holding open the lift door for her.*) Are you coming up, or not?

SARAH No, David!

DAVID What do you propose to do? Stand here shouting and bawling in the lobby? Shall I bring the porter out? Would you like him to arbitrate?

SARAH David, we are having an evening out. We are not going back to the flat.

DAVID You are having an evening out. My evening out has been ruined beyond repair.

SARAH David!

DAVID Sorry.

(*And he steps into the lift and closes the door.* SARAH *reacts with panic, not knowing what to do. Suddenly the lift door is flung open again and* DAVID *bobs out.*)

And I'll tell you another thing, the next time we go to the pictures, I choose the film.

SARAH (*pacifyingly*) All right, David.

DAVID (*driving home his advantage*) In fact, when I go to the pictures in future, I shall go on my own.

SARAH All right!

DAVID By myself.

SARAH Yes, that would suit you, wouldn't it?

DAVID And what does that mean?

SARAH Well, it saves you the trouble of inventing obscure clients from Birmingham, doesn't it?

DAVID That is over and done with.

SARAH So you say.

DAVID Look. I have not set eyes on Maxine for three months. I have stopped seeing the girl. So can we just drop that subject from our repertoire entirely? Anyway, if I did see her again I hope I could think up a better excuse than the pictures. Credit me with some imagination.

SARAH So you are still seeing her?

DAVID I am not still seeing her!

SARAH Then why do you want to go to the pictures by yourself?

DAVID Oh, for crying out——! I might as well talk to this lift shaft. (*Again opening the lift door.*) Are you coming up or not?

SARAH No, David, I want to get it settled.

DAVID I refuse to discuss anything else down here. Get in!

(SARAH, *with an upward glance, and the shrug of someone who has given up hope, steps into the lift. The door closes and we see the lift light as it moves upwards. The stage is silent. There is a tinkling laugh from behind the bedroom door. A moment's pause and then* DAVID *and* SARAH *march downstairs together.*)

All right, we'll discuss it like sensible people.

SARAH Thank you, David.

DAVID Only I want no more jibes, no more innuendoes.

SARAH No, David.

DAVID We'll sit down, quietly——

SARAH And reasonably.

DAVID —and reasonably, and we'll talk the whole thing out.

SARAH Yes, David.

(*They have crossed and entered "The Hussar."* STUART, *in his shirt-sleeves, bursts into the living-room out of the bedroom.*)

STUART I can't do it!

VALERIE (*still wearing the housecoat, follows him into the living-room*) Stuart!

STUART It's pointless, Valerie! Why don't we end this charade once and for all?

VALERIE (*sharply*) Charade? What do you mean?

STUART I know I have to close my eyes to a lot of things, but I'm not made of stone, you know. How can I make love to you with that man's pyjama case staring me in the face?

VALERIE I'm sorry. I'll move it.

STUART It's not only pyjamas. It's slippers. It's cuff-links on the dressing-table. It's his travelling clock. Possessions. Little intimate details. A briefcase. A leather-backed clothes brush.

VALERIE That's not his, it's mine as well.

STUART (*bitterly*) Togetherness. After-shave lotion. West Indian Lime. What's the matter with him, is he queer or what? No, apparently not!

VALERIE Stuart, you've got to stop!

STUART West Indian Lime! (*Slyly.*) Incidentally, did he mention it at all?

VALERIE Why—have you been using it?

STUART (*smirking*) No, no, no, no. (*Frowning again.*) Four quid a throw, eh! Expensive tastes for a man who's a self-confessed failure.

VALERIE Stop it! You're just torturing yourself.

STUART (*reflectively*) Yes. I am. I'm torturing myself. It's my nature. My personality. I'm sensitive.

VALERIE I know you are and I love you for it.

STUART That's all very well. But it's no help to me. One glimpse of a Paisley dressing-gown and I see myself for what I am: I'm a jealous man.

VALERIE No, you're not, Stuart. It's only natural.

STUART (*a cry of anguish*) What can we do?

VALERIE We do what we can. I do what *I* can. I've never told you this, Stuart, but before you come, every Friday, I take the wedding photograph off the dressing-table and I hide it. Just for you.

STUART Thank you.

VALERIE So you see, I know you're sensitive.

STUART One's got to learn to live with these things. One's got to learn to face reality. Where do you hide it?

VALERIE Oh—anywhere.

STUART Show it to me.

VALERIE Certainly not.

STUART Oh, I can take it. I have very broad shoulders. Go on, show me the wedding photograph.

VALERIE What's the point?

STUART What are you afraid of? You don't have to mollycoddle me. Show it to me. I shan't be upset because you look so radiantly happy. Everybody does on their wedding day. Why should I be upset? It's only you. Smiling. Arm in arm. (*In a sudden gust of anger.*) With that bloody raving senseless nincompoop! Come on! Where is it?

VALERIE Stuart! The neighbours!

STUART What about the neighbours! What will they think? You're having a row with your husband—"Oh, no! She never has a row with her husband. What? That lovey-dovey couple? Never go out! Sit at home every night! Drinking gin! Lights out sharp at nine! Off to bed!"

VALERIE Stuart!

STUART (*placidly*) I shall go insane. I shall go raving mad. No, face the facts, Valerie, it is more than the human frame can stand. And that's all there is to it.

VALERIE What else can I say? What else can I do?

STUART There's something.

VALERIE (*immediately on guard*) Oh?

STUART (*after a pause*) I'm just opening a can of peas here, but supposing we went away together?

VALERIE For a weekend? What would I say to David? What would you say to your wife?

STUART We'd say goodbye.

VALERIE Oh. Not for a weekend.

STUART No. For ever.

VALERIE (*after a pause*) That's completely out of the question.

STUART You might do me the courtesy of considering the idea.

VALERIE We had a pact—a firm agreement. It was the first thing we promised each other. And you were never even going to suggest it. Never.

STUART Things change, Valerie.

VALERIE Nothing's changed for us. Our situation is exactly the same and you know it! We've both got responsibilities.

STUART Liabilities.

VALERIE Responsibilities. A wife who needs you, a husband who needs me.

STUART I'm willing to give mine up.

VALERIE I'm not.

STUART I see. (*A gust of anger.*) Needs you? Where is he tonight? Don't you take any account of his movements? He's out with a woman! A woman! Needs you? Is he insatiable or what? Or are you? That's what I'm beginning to wonder!

VALERIE He needs me.

STUART He's an adulterer!

VALERIE So are you.

STUART That's different.

VALERIE That's what they all say.

STUART All? All who?

(VALERIE *turns away in disgust.*)

Very well, I'm sorry. We'll deal with specific cases. Consider your shambles of a marriage. On the one hand an attractive woman, intelligent, charming, witty, worldly, oversexed. (*Hastily.*) Sorry. Anyway, a beautiful woman. On the other hand a pathetic wreck of a man. An adulterer, a liar, a failure in life and in business. A nit.

VALERIE He's not a nit!

STUART That man has left a trail of broken businesses throughout London's West End. He's a complete failure!

VALERIE That's why I can't leave him.

STUART I just don't understand, Val. A clean break, that's all it needs. At least I could support you. At least I've got a regular job. Executive position. Expanding company. I'll be a director in two years! Firm promise! And what's he got? Nothing! Well, he must have something. (*Offhandedly.*) Just let me have a look at that wedding photograph.

VALERIE No!

STUART (*ingenuously*) No, I'm not going to criticise. I'm not going to make a scene. I'd just like to have a look at him. I'm not torturing myself. I just want to study his face. Because you can tell, do you see, from a man's facial characteristics what he's like. Whether he's intelligent, or a good businessman, or oversexed.

VALERIE Stuart, much as I love you, I'm going to hit you.

STUART Well, don't deny it! Don't say there's nothing between you! You are sleeping with your husband!

(*And* VALERIE *does hit him hard across the face. She walks into the bedroom, and comes back with his jacket and throws it at him.*)

VALERIE Out!

STUART All right, we'll discuss it like sensible people.

VALERIE Out!

(*She picks up the framed photograph of herself and raises it menacingly as* STUART *scrabbles for his coat on the floor.*)

STUART We'll sit down quietly and—ow!—— (*For* VALERIE *has stamped viciously on his hand.*) reasonably, and we'll talk the whole thing over.

VALERIE (*brandishing the photograph*) Get out!

(*He looks at her and sees that she means it. Nursing his hand, jacket under his arm, he hurries out.* VALERIE*'s temper diminishes into sadness as she lowers the photograph, looks at it and sighs. She replaces it on the small table.*

She looks around the room, picks up the two dirty glasses and goes sadly into the bedroom. At which point:

STUART *comes dejectedly down the stairs, shrugging on his jacket. He stands moodily in the foyer, lights a cigarette, looks moodily up the stairs, and then making up his mind he walks briskly over to the telephone box and enters it. At which point:*

SARAH *hurries out of "The Hussar" with the idea of using the telephone. She sees that it is occupied, and stands waiting impatiently. Meanwhile* STUART *has dialled a number.*

The telephone in the living-room rings. VALERIE, *now*

wearing her own coat, rushes out and picks up the telephone eagerly.)

Stuart?

(We hear the urgent beep-beep-beep of the S.T.D. phone. STUART *suddenly realises that he has not got a threepenny bit handy. He scrambles frantically in his pocket.)*

Hello?

*(*DAVID *comes out of "The Hussar" in a bad temper.)*

DAVID Well, are you coming home or not?

SARAH Yes. I just want to telephone my friend.

DAVID We've got a telephone at home.

(Over this STUART *has bobbed out of the telephone box, holding the bleeping instrument. He brandishes three pennies.)*

STUART Excuse me, have you got a threepenny bit?

DAVID Eh? Oh?

(And DAVID *fishes in his pockets. At which point:*
VALERIE *gives up hope of anyone answering the telephone and replaces the receiver. She picks up her handbag, takes a quick look around the living-room and goes out.*
DAVID *hands* STUART *a threepenny bit.)*

STUART Thank you.

DAVID *(to* SARAH *brusquely)* Come on!

*(*DAVID, *followed by* SARAH, *marches into the lobby.*
Meanwhile STUART, *back in the telephone box, discovers that he has been cut off.*
He jiggles the receiver rest up and down. DAVID, *who intended to take the lift, is too impatient to wait for it. With an exclamation under his breath and a jerk of his head to* SARAH *he hurries up the stairs and she follows him with a "the balloon-is-going up" look. As they disappear round the corner we see the lights of the lift descending and* VALERIE *steps out and walks away.*
Meanwhile STUART *is dialling the number again. The telephone rings in the living-room. After a few moments* DAVID, *again followed by* SARAH, *enters the living-room. Finding it empty she reacts with relief as he walks straight over to the telephone. He answers it irritably.)*

David Lord speaking!

*(*STUART *slams down the telephone and stands petrified. Then he reacts with relief at what he imagines to be a narrow escape. He goes out of the telephone box and into "The Hussar" in need of a stiff drink.* DAVID *holds the telephone for a moment and then also slams the instrument down.)*

I'm going to write to the Postmaster General.

SARAH Burglars do it to see if you are in.

(She has taken a cautious peep into the bedroom and finding it empty is completely at ease. DAVID *rubs at a drink stain on his lapel.)*

DAVID Does it leave a stain—whisky?

SARAH I wouldn't know. I've never thrown one at anybody before.

(She goes into the bedroom. DAVID *calls after her.)*

DAVID You won't throw one at me again, either—not for some time! Just to reiterate—in future I go to the pictures alone, I go for a drink alone. Are you listening? I walk alone.

*(*SARAH *reappears wearing the familiar housecoat and carrying the two glasses which she places discreetly on the drinks table.)*

SARAH You can do exactly as you please, David. Your movements are of no further interest to me.

DAVID In fact, in future, I don't see any need for any oral communication between us at all. Inside the flat or out.

SARAH Very well, David.

DAVID You lead your life, I lead mine. You have your friends, I have mine.

SARAH We know all about that.

DAVID No communication at all, with effect from—now. I have spoken my last word to my wife.

(He sits down, arms folded. SARAH, *unperturbed, also sits down and picks up a magazine. He sits watching her broodingly. After a moment—incredulously:)*

You don't just pick up a glass of Scotch in public and throw it in your husband's face! Good grief, there's got to be *some* respect in marriage! There is such a thing as human dignity! *(Lifting a half-remembered phrase from one of his Westerns.*) A man needs to—needs to walk tall among his fellow men.

SARAH Shut up, Shane.

DAVID You know that Reggie Patterson and his wife were sitting at the bar, don't you?

SARAH I couldn't care less.

DAVID You do realise that he's tentatively booked a suntrap villa in Corsica, August through September. I can see him confirming *that* booking now. What faith he is going to have in his travel agent when he's seen him with whisky streaming down his face? Suntrap villa—he'll probably think I'm fobbing him off with a pig-sty.

SARAH It is a pig-sty.

DAVID They've been converted and you know it! The pig-sties, the cow-sheds, all of them. I've never had one complaint. Apart from the so-called Sunday popular press. (*Glancing at his lapel.*) It does mark. Where's the stain remover?

(SARAH *does not reply. He continues angrily.*)

I'm talking to you!

SARAH Really? I thought you were giving it up.

DAVID (*rising*) As indeed I am. So tell me where the stain remover is and I won't trouble you again.

SARAH Bathroom.

DAVID Thank you.

(DAVID *goes out through the bedroom door.* SARAH *gets up and pours herself a drink. He reappears a moment later dabbing at his lapel with a stain remover. He applies himself to this task for a moment but his mind is elsewhere.* SARAH *sits down with her drink.*)

I say. You remember when we were down in Worthing —two three years ago?

(SARAH *glances up and notices the wide patch of stain-remover which is appearing on* DAVID*'s jacket.*)

SARAH You're putting too much on. It'll leave a stain.

DAVID Don't talk damn rot! How can a stain-remover leave a stain?

SARAH Stain-remover does leave a stain.

DAVID H'm. (*He accepts the feminine knowledge and now tries to wipe off the stain-remover with his handkerchief.)* Anyway. We went to the theatre.

SARAH (*irritably*) What theatre?

DAVID (*patiently*) In Worthing. We saw—(*He clicks his fingers, trying to recall the title.*)—that thriller.

SARAH *Gaslight!*

DAVID *Gaslight!* And incidentally, that's another play I might have mentioned. *Gaslight*, that was a very good play. (*Examining his lapel.*) Yes, it does leave a stain. *Gaslight*.

SARAH Are you feeling all right, or are you breathing in the fumes from that thing?

DAVID I'm just trying to remember the basic plot. There was this strange woman who kept hiding things—paintings, jewellery, photographs—things like that.

SARAH She didn't keep hiding things. That was the husband. (*Meaningly.*) He was trying to drive her insane.

DAVID Hmmm. What I'm getting at is, why do you keep putting our wedding photograph under the bed?

SARAH (*alarmed*) What?

DAVID It's there again. This week, last week—it's always happening.

SARAH Don't be ridiculous. You're imagining things.

(DAVID *points to* SARAH *and then to the bedroom.*)

DAVID It's there now. It's got fluff on it. Go and look.

SARAH Oh! Oh, I remember! I was looking at it.

DAVID What? Under the bed?

SARAH No, you see, I was making the bed.

DAVID (*sarcastically*) I see. It's a habit. You're making the bed. You pick up the photograph. You put it under the bed. Yes, that's logical.

SARAH If you want to know, David, I often pick up that photograph. It reminds me of happier days.

DAVID (*raising his eyebrows and speaking almost to himself*) Once more into the breach——

SARAH When I'm alone. When you're out—somewhere. I often look at that picture of us on our wedding day. When we were so happy. And I remember the things we used to do. The places we used to go to. That little Italian restaurant. Theatre Clubs.

DAVID (*softening*) We haven't been to the dogs for ages.

SARAH Classic Cinemas. The Royal Court.

DAVID Horror films, you said you liked them.

SARAH You said you liked the theatre.

DAVID I do like the theatre. Within reason. Anyway, it still doesn't explain what the photograph was doing under the bed.

SARAH How do I know! I expect it was Freudian! (*Bitterly.*) That crummy, greasy, little Italian restaurant! Spaghetti Bolognaise and take your own bottle!

DAVID I would remind you that we always took a bottle of champagne.

SARAH Yes! Portuguese! Do you know, I was looking at that photograph the other day and I was thinking that never —never in your life—have you spent more than twenty-seven and six on a meal for me. Including tip.

DAVID Rubbish!

SARAH All right. Name one. Name one lunch or dinner where you haven't had change out of thirty bob.

DAVID (*considers for a moment*) Oh—any one of a number of occasions.

SARAH Name one.

DAVID Well, one doesn't normally go into the L.S.D. of these things, but you'll recall that little celebration we had one anniversary. The bill, on that occasion, and not including tip, was in the region of six pounds eight and six.

SARAH But, David, that was for six people! (*Pause, and then bitterly.*) And that was four years ago. And then you wonder why I throw whisky in your face.

DAVID I don't wonder. I don't wonder at all. It's perfectly plain. You threw whisky in my face because of your insane jealousy over something that is over and done with.

SARAH Which just goes to show how insensitive and stupid you really are. I throw a drink in your face and you don't know why.

DAVID Because I had lunch with her from time to time—apparently.

SARAH Yes. And where did you say you had lunch?

DAVID The Caprice.

(SARAH *throws her drink in his face. A long pause.*) (*Resignedly.*) You might drop my suit in at the cleaners tomorrow.

SARAH The Caprice! Do you know how many times I've been to the Caprice? Once, in my entire life.

DAVID You wouldn't like it—it gets very crowded these days.

SARAH And what did they knock you back there for your cosy tête-à-tête lunches?

DAVID Less than you'd think. You can get in and out for a pound. (*Noting the disbelief he adds hopefully:*) Two pounds?

SARAH Very reasonable. You can take me there tomorrow.

DAVID (*hastily*) That's not including wine, of course.

SARAH It's all right. We'll take some Portuguese Champagne. The Caprice! Do you know what I have for my lunch? Do you know what I had for lunch today? Lemon curd and brown bread.

DAVID (*concerned*) You should eat a proper meal, darling.

SARAH You must have been spending a fortune on that girl! I can't afford a proper meal. I can't afford shoes, I can't afford clothes. Do you know that I've cut down the daily help to four hours a week?

DAVID Well, we are economising. At least I thought we were. (*Again rubbing his lapel.*) You've thrown five and six in my face tonight.

SARAH Where is your cheque book?

DAVID Why?

SARAH Give me your cheque book.

DAVID It's at the office.

SARAH Yes, I know it is. Under lock and key. My God, the money you must have spent! I'd like to go through your life with Maxine stub by stub. I'd like to know just how much that sordid little affair has cost. Not only on her—on yourself. Preening and primping before you go out. Preshave, after-shave, toilet water, talcum powder. Are you queer, or what? No, apparently not.

DAVID Most of those were gifts—from airlines and so forth.

SARAH (*ignoring this*) The aftershave alone costs four pounds a bottle. Because I've seen it in a window in Bond Street.

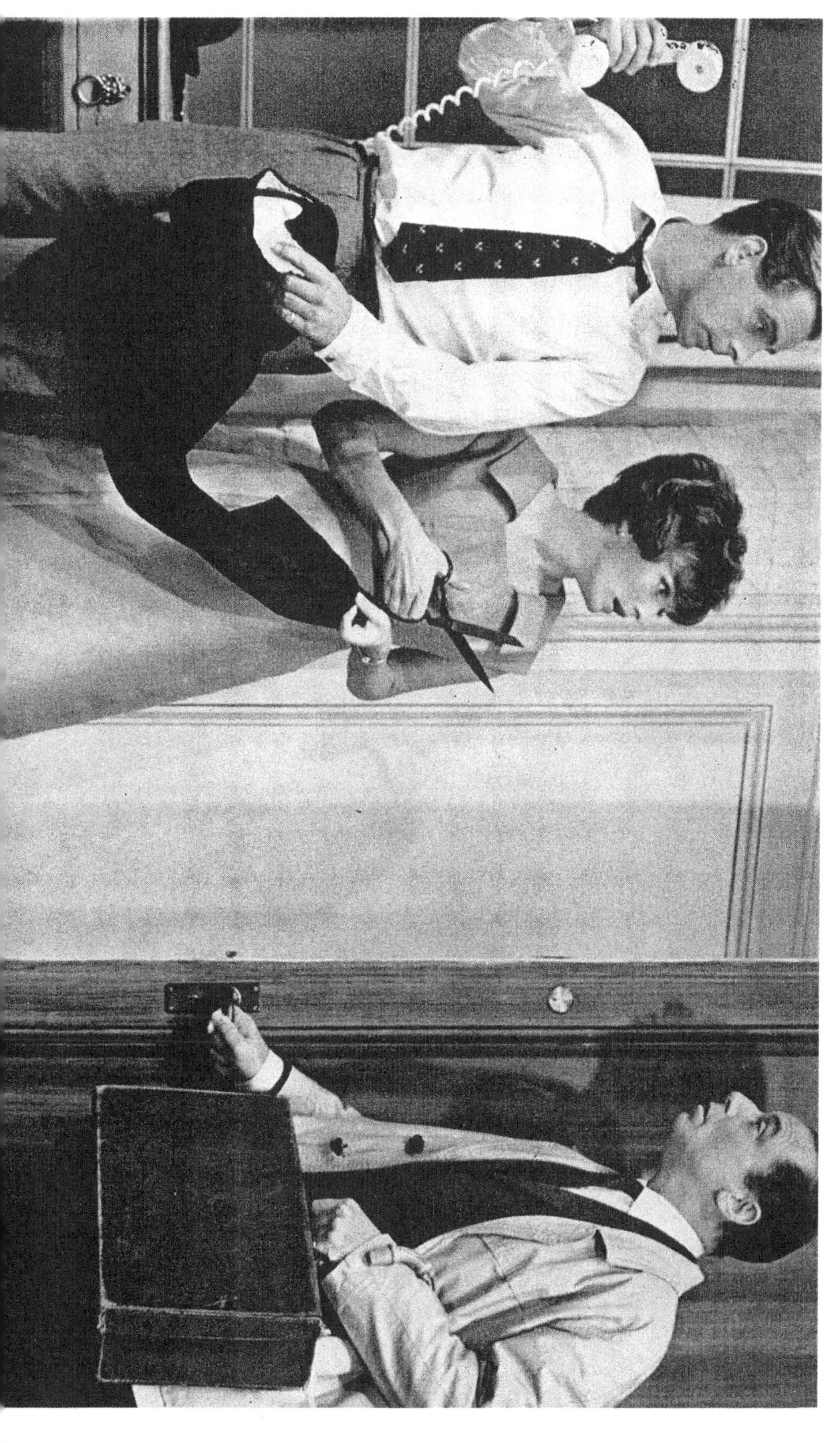

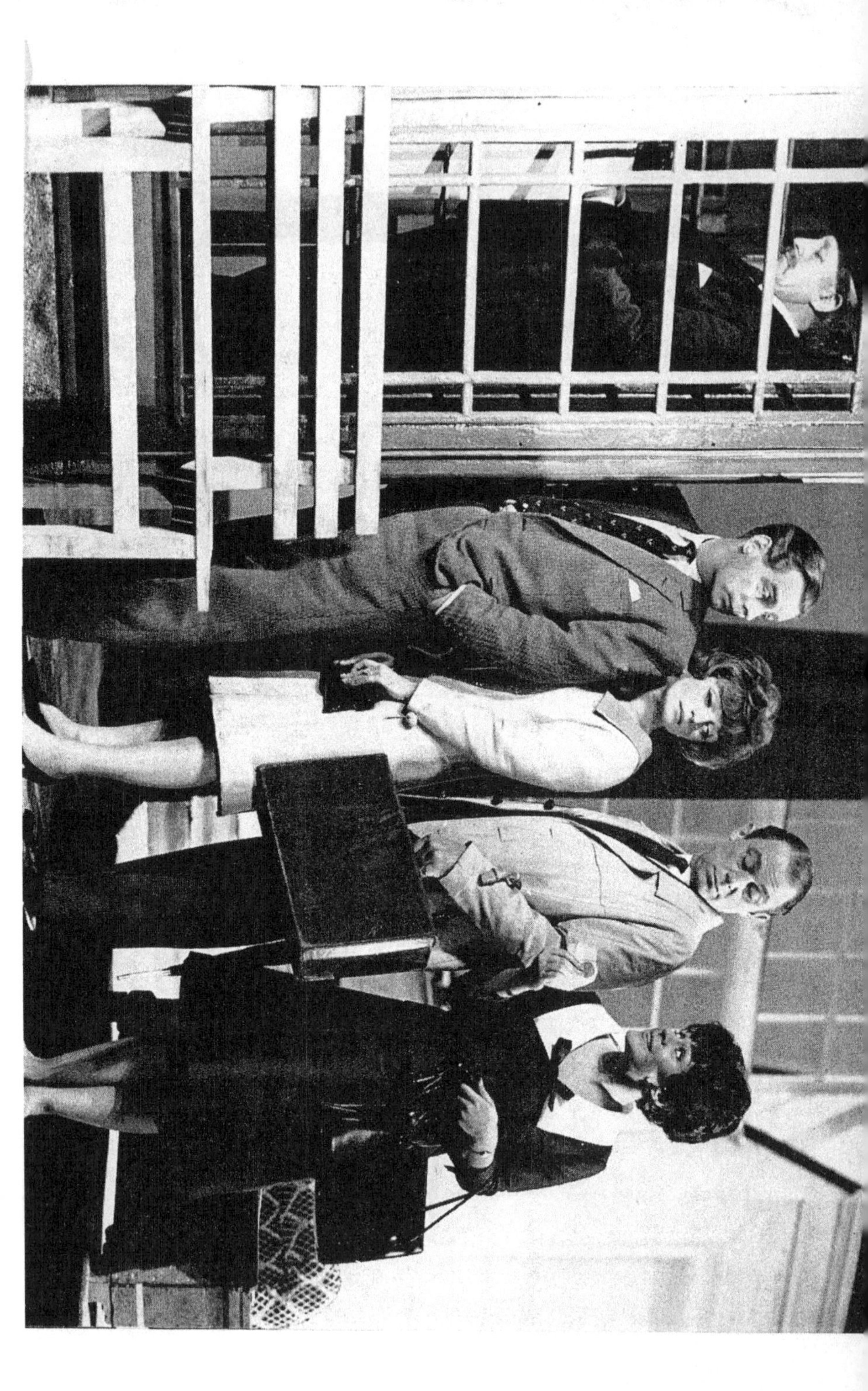

DAVID Ah, well, there you have me. I don't know the cost. That happened to be a present.

SARAH And where did she get the money? Is she on the game or something?

DAVID A particularly coarse remark. As a matter of fact it was a present from the Malta Tourist Office. They had a particularly good year last year. And if you don't believe me you can look in my briefcase and read their annual report. And, incidentally, *while* on the subject of the briefcase and *while* on the subject of the aftershave lotion, who poured the latter into the former?

SARAH What are you talking about?

DAVID I haven't mentioned it before, because it seemed such a spiteful, cheap and jealous little action. But I'd like to tell you that I'm well aware that last Friday night you deliberately poured at least ten shillings' worth of West Indian Lime into my briefcase.

SARAH I did what?

DAVID Good grief! Women and their petty little minds! Can't you rise to anything? Can't you rise to any occasion? At all? Haven't you any imagination? Any zest for life?

SARAH What life?

DAVID Life as it's lived! The throbbing world we live in! Men—— take—— women——! And you have to drag it down to your own suburban, superficial little level!

SARAH What do you want me to do? Cut my wrists?

DAVID Yes! A gesture! (*Prudently.*) Well, you don't have to go as far as that. But at least let's get this affair outside the realm of the household account book! I took the girl to a restaurant. Is that all that matters? That the bill came to four pounds?

(SARAH *is astounded—speechless with rage.*)

What about the conversations? The unity between that girl and me? The electricity between us? Doesn't that interest you at all? Doesn't it fascinate you?

SARAH Four pounds! Four pounds for a meal! For two! While I—— (*She looks at him for a moment, again lost for words.*) Four pounds! Four pounds for a meal! Four pounds for a bottle of pansy scent! Four pounds for this! Four pounds for that!

(*And in a fit of rage* SARAH *sweeps into the bedroom.* DAVID, *feeling himself the victor, is pleased.*)

DAVID (*to himself*) Woman—the immortal pigmy. (*And pleased with this also, he goes to pour himself a drink, repeating his* mot.) Woman—the immortal pigmy.

(*He pours himself the drink and stands beaming patronisingly at the photograph of* VALERIE. *It is some moments before he realises that he is looking at the portrait of a total stranger. He reacts, looks closer at it and then, mystified, turns instinctively towards the bedroom door for an explanation. But at this moment there is a resounding crash as we hear* SARAH *throw his aftershave lotion on the floor of the bathroom. As she follows this with other unguents,* DAVID, *alarmed, hurries into the bedroom.*)

If that's my West Indian Lime——

(*The rest is lost as he slams the door behind him. Upon which* VALERIE *hurries into the lobby and steps into the lift. From the bedroom we hear the muffled row, screams and crashes.* VALERIE *hurries into the living-room and immediately reacts as she realises that* DAVID *and* SARAH *are at home. Quickly and quietly she takes the photograph of* SARAH *from her handbag and replaces it on the table. She takes her own photograph from the table and hurries out of the room. Immediately the bedroom door is flung open, and* DAVID, *clutching to his breast the few toilet articles he has managed to salve from the wreckage, stalks into the room, followed by* SARAH.)

Like living in a bloody madhouse. I don't know what the hell's got into you—I don't know what the hell's going on in this place. And another thing—(*Pointing accusingly at the photograph with his free hand.*)—who's that?

SARAH It's me, you fool!

(DAVID, *still clutching his precious bottles and sprays, crosses and peers at the photograph. He looks at his wife to check the resemblance.*)

DAVID H'm.

SARAH (*anxiously*) Isn't it?

DAVID (*airily*) What? Yes, yes, yes.

(*He carefully puts down his bottles and sprays one by one. During the above* VALERIE *has come slowly down the steps and now wanders rather sadly across to "The Hussar", where she sits pensively on the bench outside.* DAVID *carefully dusts his hands and checks his bottles.*)

Right. All present and correct except the West Indian Lime, Sandalwood talc and the jar of shaving cream which happily for you was almost empty. (*He looks abstractedly at the photograph again.*)

SARAH I shall smash them all before I've finished.

DAVID (*absently*) I doubt it, I very much doubt it.

SARAH (*quietly and sadly*) Every single one. (*A pause, and then very sadly, dreaming of lost opportunities.*) I heard of a woman who cut the sleeves off all her husband's suits.

DAVID (*still absently*) Bit vicious, that.

SARAH Except for his golfing jacket. She left him his golfing jacket.

DAVID That was a mistake.

SARAH Yes. He went off with a lady golfer.

DAVID Yes. He would have done. (*He broods for a moment and then looks at the photograph again.*) Well, it could be the subconscious. I've heard of cases. Jungle, places like that.

SARAH Now what?

DAVID Well, there is always a rational explanation. You see something. It doesn't register. But it's stamped indelibly —up there—the subconscious. The inner mind.

SARAH (*accusingly*) Have you been reading a book again?

DAVID And then—don't interrupt my train of thought—and then you look at a photograph, an ordinary photograph of your wife, and your subconscious says: "Just a minute, old boy, there's something fishy here."

SARAH What are you rambling about?

DAVID At some period, I don't know when, there has been on that spot a photograph of somebody else. I've got it in my subconscious.

SARAH (*nervously*) You're imagining things.

DAVID Oh, no. I didn't imagine the wedding photograph under

the bed, did I? I didn't imagine my pyjama case in the bath. I didn't put it there, you didn't put it there. Who did?

SARAH (*tentatively and hopefully*) Poltergeists?

(*As* DAVID *speaks he begins prowling round the flat, looking for evidence.*)

DAVID And something else. Two weeks ago when we went out that door was quite specifically open. When we came back it was quite specifically shut.

SARAH How on earth can you remember that?

DAVID I do remember. I quite specifically left it open to circulate the air. If these flats have a fault it's that the ventilation ducts aren't sufficiently—— (*Triumphantly.*) Ah! (*He has picked up a cigarette end from an ashtray.*) Exhibit "A". Well, come on. You don't smoke and I don't wear lipstick.

SARAH You wear everything else.

DAVID I'm waiting.

SARAH All right. I lent the flat to someone.

DAVID Did you indeed?

SARAH It's not a crime, is it? I lent it to a friend.

DAVID What friend?

SARAH A girl friend.

DAVID Which girl friend?

SARAH Just a girl friend. You don't know her. A nice girl. Educated. Very respectable.

DAVID What does she do?

SARAH She's an analytical chemist. I just lent her the flat.

DAVID What for? Experiments?

SARAH In a way.

DAVID Come on, then. Why did you lend her the flat?

SARAH (*in a small voice*) To commit adultery.

DAVID Ah! Well, that's all right. I thought perhaps she was committing some minor infringement of the lease. We have to watch these things. Keep on the right side of the law. But, no, we're in the clear. We're only running a brothel.

SARAH (*shocked*) David!

DAVID Yes, that appeals to me. I work my way up. Solid business, successful man. Flat in South Kensington. Five hundred a year plus rates. And what happens. You turn it into a red lamp area.

SARAH David, she's a nice girl!

DAVID She sounds it. A nice, educated, very respectable adulteress. Given the free run of my home.

SARAH Good heavens, she won't contaminate it! Anyway, she's not an adulteress. It's the adulterer she commits adultery with. She's single.

DAVID Single and fancy free. Well, what's wrong with her own little nest? Why doesn't she commit adultery there?

SARAH She can't. It's not convenient.

DAVID Oh? Narrow-minded Victorian fuddy-duddy landlady or what?

SARAH She shares a flat with five girls.

DAVID I see. And how long has she been committing it here?

SARAH Not long.

DAVID How long?

SARAH Not long. Only three months.

DAVID (*outraged*) Three months!

SARAH (*in her small voice*) Yes. Every Friday.

DAVID What! All these Fridays! When you've been dragging me out to Italian film Festivals, French *avant garde*, and all that foreign tripe and rubbish! And why? You've been stuffing sub-titles down my throat week after week so that some cheap little slut can bounce up and down on my bed!

SARAH For the last time, Valerie is a nice, respectable, educated——

DAVID I'm not interested in her "O" levels. It's her activities here that we're concerned with. Where does she find these men? Do you procure them for her or does she pick them up?

SARAH Not men. A man. And she didn't pick him up. He picked —(*Correcting herself.*) met her.

(*During the following,* VALERIE *gets up and wanders away. Almost immediately* STUART *wanders out of "The Hussar", gin and tonic in hand, cigar in his mouth, and gazes expansively out at the world. He preens himself, in his own mind very much the successful man.*)

DAVID And what's he? Some kind of gigolo or what?

SARAH You've got a foul mind!

DAVID Foul mind for a foul subject. I know these fellows. Their minds never rise above their navels. All brawn, no brain. Coal-heavers, that class. Certain types of merchant seamen.

SARAH He's not like that at all! From all I gather he's quite nice.

DAVID Educated and respectable, no doubt?

SARAH Yes. He's a businessman. He insures things.

DAVID (*slightly mollified*) Oh. Well, thank heaven for small mercies. And why am I extending my hospitality to him? What's his burden in life? Does he share a flat with five girls?

SARAH No, the thing is, he's married.

DAVID Ah! One of those.

SARAH (*sharply*) Yes, David. One of those.

DAVID Don't change the subject. Admitting my own indiscretions, at least I've not commandeered the home of a total stranger as if it were a back room in Paris.

SARAH I don't see it like that at all. I look upon Stuart almost as an old friend.

DAVID Stuart? Stuart who? And when have you had the pleasure of his services?

SARAH I've never even met him. Just that Valerie's talked a lot about him.

DAVID Ah! Vivid descriptions. Erotica.

SARAH Don't be more oafish than you can help. (*A pause.*) It's quite sad really—Stuart's little life.

DAVID Sad! The man's got everything going for him. A rent-free apartment. An oversexed ego. An oversexed mistress. Free booze. Do you know what he'd have to pay, by the hour, for a place like this?

SARAH He couldn't afford it. He's not one of these self-employed tycoons who go lording it about the Caprice.

DAVID Anyway, what am I supposed to do? Leave him out a bowl of hot soup?

SARAH You might stop sneering. At least he does hold down a regular job. At least he's got some sort of security.

DAVID Oh, yes, we know these nine to five Lotharios. Sit polishing their backsides on an office chair all day, grabbing their seedy comforts in the evenings.

SARAH Why? Is promiscuity all right so long as you stamp your own insurance card?

DAVID At least I do have guts! I do grab at opportunities! I do seize life with both hands! And who's this girl? You have some very strange friends. Is she ill? Is she mentally unbalanced?

(During the above STUART *has strolled back into "The Hussar".)*

SARAH She's a normal healthy girl!

DAVID Normal? Healthy? Crawling about on her hands and knees in a strange flat! Sliding photographs under beds! Hurling pyjama cases about! Closing doors that have been specifically left open! Do you call that normal and healthy?

SARAH No. But she has to do these things. You see, she's pretending to be married.

DAVID She's perverted. What kick does she get out of that then? Why does she pretend to be married?

SARAH Because she's independent. She doesn't want Stuart to leave his wife. She doesn't want to get involved.

DAVID *(resignedly)* Well, it takes all sorts. Who am I to judge? I won't condemn your eccentric friend. Just keep her out of the flat in future. That's all I ask.

SARAH *(meekly)* Yes, David.

DAVID There'll be no more Fridays. No more classics, culture, continental garbage.

SARAH No, David.

DAVID Very well then. So long as that's completely understood.

SARAH Yes, David.

*(*DAVID, *having got his victory, is in better humour. Shaking his head, he allows himself to muse benignly on the ways of women.)*

DAVID It baffles me. Pretending to be married. Puzzling are the ways of woman. Woman—the immortal sphinx.

SARAH Yes, David.

DAVID Who's she supposed to be married to?

SARAH You, David.

DAVID Woman—the immortal—— (*A double-take.*) Me!

SARAH I believe so.

DAVID Me! Her husband! This crazy woman! Let loose—in South Kensington! What's she doing, what's she saying? Outside Harrods. Saturday morning. "Want a good time, dearie? I'm Mrs David Lord."

SARAH It's only to him!

(DAVID, *ignoring* SARAH, *storms across to the telephone.*)

DAVID I shall ring the police. It's a C.I.D. matter. She wants locking up.

SARAH Don't be ridiculous.

DAVID (*picking up the telephone*) No, no. I should be failing in my duty as a citizen. Don't worry, she won't go to prison. They're given care and attention in these enlightened times.

SARAH She didn't mean any harm.

DAVID (*slamming the phone down*) Harm! What's she doing to my image in the world of business? I shall take out an injunction against her. I shall ring my solicitor. (*He picks up the telephone directory, and, flicking through it, wanders about the room.*) Baldwin—Baldwin, Baldwin. Baldwin D. Baldwin E.

SARAH You can't ring him.

DAVID I shall ring him. Here we are—Baldwin, Malcolm. Commissioner for Oaths.

SARAH Because you still owe him money. For that trouble over the Portuguese Champagne.

DAVID (*accepting this fact he slams the telephone directory shut*) That woman does not enter this flat again. Is that clear?

SARAH Yes, David.

DAVID You will never see her again. You'll never speak to her, you will never write to her. You will not communicate with her in any way at all.

SARAH No, David.

DAVID She does not ever—whatever the circumstances—set foot on these premises at all.

(*But over the above* VALERIE *has entered, walked into the telephone box and dialled. She is upset. The telephone in the living-room rings.*)

SARAH (*picking up the telephone*) No, David. Hello?

(VALERIE *pushes home the threepenny bit and gabbles into the telephone.*)

VALERIE Sarah, I've got to see you. I'm just outside. I'm coming round now.

(*She replaces the telephone before* SARAH *has a chance to reply.*)

SARAH Only the whole point is, she's coming round now.

DAVID If she comes, I go.

SARAH But she's coming!

DAVID It's my flat! Tell her! She's barred!

SARAH She's my friend.

DAVID I'm your husband.

SARAH She's upset!

DAVID *I'm* upset!

SARAH I can't stop her.

(DAVID *draws himself up to his full height and walks to the door.*)

DAVID I shall send for my things tomorrow.

(*And he walks out. Over the above* VALERIE *has entered the lobby, pressed the button for the lift and got into it.* SARAH, *finding herself still holding the telephone, puts it down.* DAVID *charges down the stairs, storms across and into "The Hussar".* SARAH, *anticipating* VALERIE*'s arrival, opens the door as* VALERIE *enters.*)

SARAH Come in. He's gone out.

VALERIE I've lost Stuart.

SARAH He's in a filthy mood. He's found out.

VALERIE He just stormed off and left me.

SARAH You can't stay long. He's left home. He'll be back any minute.

(*During the following* STUART, *carrying another drink, wanders out of "The Hussar" and sits on the bench.*)

VALERIE Stuart won't. It's for ever this time. (*A cry from the heart.*) What's wrong with me?

SARAH They don't understand women.

VALERIE I've given that man everything. I've schemed, plotted, fabricated—I've lied to him week after week. And what thanks do I get? Nothing.

SARAH We pamper them too much. I threw a drink at him tonight and it meant nothing to him.

VALERIE He's no gratitude.

SARAH He's no imagination.

VALERIE It's not as if I enjoyed lying. There's no pleasure in it. There's no end to it. Sarah, last week I had to invent a whole mother-in-law—cottage in the Cotswolds, white hair, apple cheeks, the lot, and all he said was "She sounds a right old cow".

SARAH You can't win.

VALERIE God, what a wonderful world we'd have if only men would accept us for what we are!

SARAH (*demurring*) Well, you must admit that yours is rather a special case.

VALERIE Why? Because I'm honest?

SARAH Honest!

VALERIE But I am, Sarah! I'm honest with myself. I love Stuart, but I can't bear the thought of having him under my feet all day. I don't want marriage. I don't want evenings out, evenings at home, breakfasts, anniversaries, toothbrushes nestling side by side. Togethernesss. Forgive me, Sarah, but I don't want—(*Looking round the room.*)—all this.

SARAH (*tartly, taking offence*) What do you want?

VALERIE Sex. In moderation. Well, why not? I'm normal, healthy. I'm a woman. Aren't I?

SARAH Yes.

VALERIE What's wrong with that? What's this simple naive thing that men have got about women? Why do they only put us into two categories? You're either a hausfrau or a nymphomaniac.

SARAH You've invented a category of your own.

VALERIE But I don't enjoy it.

SARAH Yes, you do.

VALERIE No, I don't! Coming round here—putting on your clothes—putting out my photograph—talking about "our" husband?

SARAH You don't do it very well.

VALERIE What do you mean?

SARAH I've told you, Valerie. David's found out. It's your own fault, darling. I know that you tidy up every Friday, and you do it beautifully, but after all, you did leave my wedding photograph under the bed—three weeks in a row.

VALERIE Oh, damn! I swear that in future——

SARAH There isn't going to be any future. It's more than my marriage is worth. Anyway, you say it's all over with Stuart. Why don't you find yourself a nice, uncomplicated single man?

VALERIE Because they don't exist. Married or single—they're complicated. And I want Stuart. I love him.

SARAH But he's married.

VALERIE That doesn't matter to me. It only matters to him. Why are men such romantics! Why can't they simply get involved? Why can't they get involved, and be involved and stay involved? Why do we have to have their wild, romantic, useless gestures? Throwing themselves into rivers, carving initials on trees.

SARAH (*wistfully*) I wish David would throw himself into a river.

VALERIE He will if you drive him to it. They'll all have a go at it sooner or later.

SARAH No, he would for Maxine. But not for me.

VALERIE I thought that was all over.

SARAH It is. But I can't forget it. I can't get it out of my mind.

VALERIE Poor Sarah.

SARAH (*brightening*) Oh, no! It's lovely! I can be such a complete bitch! About anything! There's one marvellous thing about infidelity—it puts a complete end to this farce of give and take in marriage. Oh, we've had rows before—I'm always starting them. But men never really enjoy them, and then they sulk and you have to apologise. But when they're unfaithful—well, you can't put a foot wrong.

VALERIE You're not *pleased* about Maxine?

SARAH (*truthfully*) Broken-hearted. But look at the situation. It's the only opportunity I've had to be the perfect woman. I can be obnoxious, illogical, unreasonable and deliriously outrageous. I can spit at him, throw drinks at him, make a fool of him in public. I can fling my wedding ring across a restaurant and he's the one who has to grovel for it. I feel so female. I feel like Catherine the Great.

VALERIE (*now wistful herself*) I miss all that—being single.

SARAH You miss all kinds of things! I never give him a minute! And the best part is, he never knows when I'm going to strike next. Three o'clock in the morning! I woke up—some sound in the street. I looked at David all curled up and sleeping like a child. So I belted him with his travelling clock.

VALERIE (*giggling*) Poor David!

SARAH (*also giggling*) Poor David! And every time he leaves home he never gets further than the pub.

(*At which point* DAVID *wanders out of "The Hussar", nursing a drink and looking sorry for himself. He and* STUART *disregard each other.*)

He moons about outside, feeling sorry for himself. And thinking he's got a minute's peace. But there's the phone box outside and I ring him up. Every time he thinks I'll say I'm sorry. But I don't. I swear at him!

VALERIE Is he there now?

SARAH Of course he is!

VALERIE Are you going to ring him?

SARAH Oh, it's such a shame! Shall I?

VALERIE Yes!

SARAH (*picking up the phone and dialling*) What shall I say?

VALERIE What do you usually say?

SARAH I don't know. It just comes out.

(*As* SARAH *dials the last digit,* DAVID *looks at his empty glass and wanders back into "The Hussar". The phone in the telephone box rings.* STUART *looks across at it with some surprise. He looks around, and then approaches it gingerly. He enters the telephone box and lifts up the telephone.*)

SARAH You foul, filthy, dirty, adulterous pig!

(*And she slams the telephone down.* SARAH *and* VALERIE *go off into a fit of giggling.* STUART *holds the telephone and looks into the mouthpiece, amazed. He speaks nervously into the telephone.*)

STUART Hello?

(*He puts down the telephone and goes back to his bench, visibly shaken. He sits brooding over his drink.*)

VALERIE What else do you do?

SARAH Anything. Throw things, lock him out. Anything. (*They both sit thinking of something to do to* DAVID.) I did hear of a woman who cut all the sleeves off her husband's suits.

VALERIE (*goading*) You wouldn't dare.

SARAH Perhaps not.

VALERIE Would you?

(*They sit looking at each other. Then they burst out giggling again and simultaneously rush into the bedroom.* DAVID *walks out of the "The Hussar" with a drink and this time sits on the bench next to* STUART. *There is a moment before* STUART *opens up a pub conversation with a stranger.*)

STUART Quite pleasant now.

DAVID Yes. Rain keeps off.

STUART Quite warm. (*Pause.*) 'Strordinary thing just happened.

DAVID Really.

STUART (*points to the telephone box with his drink*) Public call box. Just rang. Answered it. Some woman hurls abuse at me.

DAVID Ah, that would have been for me.

STUART (*politely*) Oh, I see. (*Pause.*) Funny things, phone boxes. Often wondered—why do they print the instructions in Spanish?

DAVID Well, you'd be surprised at the number of Spanish visitors we do get. To these shores.

STUART Is that a fact?

DAVID Oh, yes! Au pair girls alone. (*Pause.*) No, we live just round the corner. This is the local, so far as I'm concerned. Quite handy, really. She often rings me up. Sunday lunch ready. Report back. Quite handy.

STUART That's quite handy.

DAVID Oh, yes! Of course, what you just caught was the brunt of a marital tiff.

STUART (*nodding*) Ah! There but for the grace of God——

DAVID Well—they have to let off steam. Keeps them quiet.

STUART We all go through it.

DAVID I always feel sorry for these dreary suburban couples who plod on, year after year, without so much as a cross word. And they boast about it.

STUART Oh, well, it's your suburban mind. Your suburban attitude. Suburban mediocrity.

DAVID The nine-to-five brigade. Rush-hour chumps. Little semis, little gardens, little wives. (*Delicately.*) Do you live in Town, by the way?

STUART Oh, yes. Absolute necessity. After all, this is where life is lived, isn't it? It's the hub. Restaurants.

DAVID Theatres.

STUART (*thinking hard*) Exhibitions.

DAVID Night life.

STUART The female of the species——

DAVID More deadly than the male. (*The ice completely broken,* DAVID *can now speak freely.*) Yes, the brunt of a marital tiff. My own stupid fault. Getting too involved, that was my trouble.

STUART The old showdown. I've still got that to come—touch wood.

DAVID (*musing*) Beautiful girl! Beautiful. Eighteen years old. Yes, she's a petrol pump attendant.

STUART Oh, yes.

DAVID Wonderful girl. Convent education. Father in Harley Street. She could have been anything. Petrol pump attendant. It amuses her. A girl with less guts would have gone and worked in Harrods.

STUART Sounds a wonderful girl.

DAVID I fell in love with her. I'm not ashamed of it. I fell in love. I'm not talking about your twopenny ha'penny affairs. I was besotted. I tried to keep it in line. I know one's got to be careful. Discreet little bistros. Out of the way pubs. But it wasn't enough. Do you know what true happiness is? I'll tell you what true happiness is. Being seen by other people. To walk down Coventry Street—together. Exuding love. To sit in a public restaurant, holding hands. To introduce her to one's friends. By Jove, it's a wonderful feeling. I went too far. I couldn't stop myself. I took her round to meet the wife's sister. Then the lot came out. I suppose it was bound to, looking back.

STUART So the balloon went up?

DAVID (*with feeling*) What! (*Indicating the phone box.*) You heard for yourself—and that's been going on for three months.

(STUART, *with a sharp intake of breath, raps the bench.*)

What?

STUART I was just saying. Touch wood.

DAVID Same problem?

STUART Worse than that. Mine's married.

(DAVID *instinctively duplicates* STUART'*s gesture—the sharp intake of breath and the rap on wood.*)

DAVID Is the husband, er—aware?

STUART (*disparagingly*) No! The man's a complete twit. Typical cuckold figure. Paint it in letters three feet high and he wouldn't see it. The man's barely literate, anyway.

DAVID What—artisan? That class?

STUART (*shocked*) Oh, no! He is a businessman—thank God. She's an educated girl, after all. No, big business. He's got the ambitions of a tycoon—but unfortunately the brain and mental agility of a coal heaver.

DAVID (*nods knowingly*) Big chap?

STUART No, scrawny, seedy, weedy little blighter. Not that I've met him.

DAVID Extraordinary, isn't it—how these ugly beggars always get the best women. Chap I was hearing about only tonight—some little rabbit, seedy little office clerk and there's this girl raving for him. Screaming for it. Nice, educated girl—friend of my wife's—and she makes the most extraordinary arrangements to—er—satisfy him.

STUART Extraordinary.

DAVID Women, eh? The immortal sphinx.

STUART That's rather good.

DAVID (*brooding*) How many husbands have been driven into pubs tonight because they've crossed swords with the immortal sphinx?

STUART Very good.

DAVID How do we stand it? It's a wonder we don't all throw ourselves in the river. Why won't they let us get married and be married and stay married? We wouldn't need other women then. Why do they want their marriages to be one perpetual honeymoon? What are they afraid of? Why do they have to stand around in little black dresses at six o'clock every evening? They don't want marriage. They want a life-long cocktail party for two. Sliced lemon. Ice all over the kitchen floor. Hairdressers' jokes. And the ashtrays full of nuts. Did you ever see a film called *Woman In a Dressing Gown?*

STUART No, I missed that one.

DAVID By Jove, how I'd love to be married to a woman like that! The perfect slut.

STUART All women are sluts at heart. Kleenex in the bed.

DAVID Dressing table like a sump pit.

STUART Woman—the immortal slut.

DAVID But why won't they accept it? Why do they have to spend so much time and effort keeping a marriage together, before it's even falling apart? If they'd only relax —so would we. We wouldn't need other women.

STUART If only they'd realise that men are monogamous.

DAVID That's true! It's very true! Man is monogamous! We don't enjoy the bother and expense of running two women. They drive us to it. Yes, it's very true.

STUART (*preening himself*) True and insoluble. If only one had the guts to decide on one woman and stick to her.

DAVID If only in fairness to the other one.

STUART Quite.

DAVID I mean the one one isn't sticking to.

STUART (*indicating* DAVID'*s glass*) Quite. Fancy the other half in there?

DAVID Ahhh—I ought to get back really.

STUART Not even a quick one?

DAVID Well, why not? Give her time to cool off.

(*They have moved into "The Hussar". As they do so* VALERIE *and* SARAH *bound out of the bedroom, carrying a pair of scissors each.* SARAH *also carries a jacket.*)

SARAH (*happily*) It's terrifying! I can't stop myself!

VALERIE It's like a disease! It's therapeutic!

SARAH What a pity it's nearly over.

VALERIE The last one. Right sleeve or left?

SARAH Either.

(They take the jacket between them and each begin to hack away at a sleeve.)

VALERIE *(reciting with childish delight)* And here comes a chopper —to—chop—off—your—sleeve!

VALERIE / SARAH *(together)* { Chop! Chop! Chop! / Snip! Snip! Snip!

(And the jacket falls to the floor leaving them both holding a sleeve in one hand and a pair of scissors in the other. SARAH *is suddenly deflated.)*

SARAH It's all over.

VALERIE *(still buoyant)* What about his dressing-gown?

SARAH *(sadly)* I've already done his dressing-gown.

VALERIE His shirts! His sweaters!

SARAH The wool would unravel.

VALERIE His pyjamas!

SARAH I think we've gone too far.

VALERIE You're supposed to go too far! Don't you remember—you're Catherine the Great!

SARAH He'll go raving mad. *(Looking at the sleeve fondly.)* I've just ruined my marriage.

VALERIE Rubbish!

SARAH Yes, I have.

VALERIE Anyway, what about me? I've just been divorced from your husband. Think of all the bother I'm going to have. Finding another flat, for one thing.

SARAH All these weeks I've had him in the palm of my hand. And I've thrown it all away for five minutes' pleasure.

VALERIE *(thinking hard)* How's Monica's marriage? She might co-operate. Lovely flat in Mount Street. Husband at sea. That's a help. These Fridays were rather cramping.

SARAH That's right, pull the ladder up.

VALERIE Oh, Sarah! He'll forgive you. After all, you did it because you love him.

SARAH He'll leave me.

VALERIE He won't leave you!

SARAH It's all right for you. You've still got Stuart.

VALERIE How have I got Stuart? He's walked out.

SARAH He'll come back.

VALERIE Come back where? Monica's flat in Mount Street, husband commanding a nuclear submarine? He'll think I'm a bigamist. No, I'm the one with the real problem, Sarah. I've got to start completely from scratch. New flat. New husband. New lover to find. Hanging about outside the Reform Club. Loitering in bookshops. Getting accosted. It's no fun for me.

(SARAH *has picked up the jacket and, cradling it, is stroking it lovingly. She has not been listening to* VALERIE.)

SARAH Poor David! At least I might have left him this. His business suit. It's like cutting off his bread and butter. Poor sleeveless David!

VALERIE He'll be sitting in his office like the Venus de Milo.

SARAH I wish I could sew them on for him again—like Wendy and Peter Pan's shadow. And then we'd be happy. The—the——! (*For over the above, while stroking the coat, she has discovered a note in one of the pockets and taken it out and glanced at it.*) He's still seeing her! "Thank you for the darling lunch——" (*Incredulously.*) At the Mirabelle! (*She flings the jacket across the room.*) That does it. Valerie—I'm leaving him.

(*She marches into the bedroom.* VALERIE *runs after her.*)

VALERIE Darling, there could be a quite simple explanation——

(*As the bedroom door closes* STUART *and* DAVID *emerge from "The Hussar".*)

DAVID Yes, old boy, I see it very clearly now. Man is a monogamous animal. I shall give up the girl completely.

STUART I can't give mine up. I've made the decision. I shall leave my wife.

DAVID I shall ring up the wife at once. I agree with her. I've been a foul, filthy, dirty adulterous pig.

STUART Yes, that's what I shall do, and then I shall go round and confront the husband, man to man. "Sir, I am in love with your wife." She'll have to marry me then.

DAVID (*shaking his hand*) Good luck, old chap.

STUART Good hunting.

(STUART, *putting his shoulders back to face his ordeal, goes off.* DAVID, *also putting his shoulders back, steps over to the telephone box and fishes for a threepenny bit.*

SARAH, *carrying a suitcase, flounces out of the bedroom, followed by* VALERIE.)

VALERIE Sarah, you *can't* stay with Monica! You'll ruin my entire life!

SARAH I shall stay with whom I please. And I'm going to ring him up now at the pub and tell him I'm leaving, the foul, filthy, dirty adulterous pig.

SARAH *picks up the telephone.* DAVID *has entered the telephone box and also picked up the telephone. They both begin to dial in exact unison. The engaged signal sounds.*

CURTAIN

ACT II

Thirty minutes later.
DAVID *and* SARAH *are still trying to get through to each other. As they dial,* DAVID *is leaning hopelessly against the wall of the telephone box.* SARAH *is lolling in a chair.* VALERIE *is reading a magazine. The engaged signal sounds again and they both put their telephones down.* DAVID *now has a drink with him and he walks out of the box with it, stretching his legs.*

SARAH It's him. He's talking to her. I can tell. Half an hour he's been talking to her. I'll kill him. I'll kill myself.
(VALERIE *ignores this.*)
Valerie!

VALERIE (*lowering her magazine*) If you go and stay with Monica I shall never speak to you again. (*She returns to her magazine.*)

SARAH I'm not going to stay with anybody. I'm going to kill myself. I wonder if I can get the operator to interrupt the call.
(*She picks up the telephone again.* DAVID *goes back into the telephone box and picks up his telephone. We feel that the stalemate is going to be repeated. Then* DAVID *realises that he has left his drink on the bench outside "The Hussar". Putting down the telephone he goes out to collect it as* SARAH *dials. The telephone rings and* DAVID *hurries back into the box.*)

SARAH (*to* VALERIE) Got him!
(DAVID *picks up the telephone.*)

DAVID Hello? Hello? Sarah?

SARAH (*bitter-sweet*) Hello, David.

DAVID Darling, I've been trying to get you for half an hour!

SARAH (*still bitter-sweet*) Have you? Oh, dear me. But darling, why didn't you come home?

DAVID Well, I was going to come home, darling, but I was just sitting outside and I was thinking, and it suddenly struck me that I don't take you out often enough.

SARAH Darling, how thoughtful.

DAVID (*encouraged*) Yes. And I thought what an excellent idea it would be if you were to join me down here and we popped off to the Caprice. For a bite of dinner.

SARAH Darling! Or the Mirabelle?

DAVID Or the Mira—— what?

SARAH You haven't been entirely frank with me, have you, David?

DAVID (*taking a deep breath*) Well, I'm glad it's all out in the open because, funnily enough, I'd decided only tonight to make a clean——

SARAH (*venomously*) I hate you! I loathe you! Do you hear me? I hate your guts! I despise you!

(VALERIE *has lowered her magazine and is listening with interest.*)

DAVID And with good reason, darling.

SARAH You ought to be locked up! There ought to be places for people like you! Settlements! Penal colonies!

DAVID I agree with you. Whole-heartedly.

SARAH I'd like to kick you!

DAVID I can understand that, but——

SARAH All these weeks! All these lies! Tonight! All the time you were sniggering to yourself! What a good joke to tell Maxine! That's all I am to you! A funny story over coffee! At two shillings a cup!

VALERIE That's very good!

SARAH You shut up!

DAVID I'm not saying anything, darling.

SARAH And you shut up as well! I'm going to destroy you, David. I'm going to destroy everything you possess! Everything! Do you hear me!

DAVID Now, darling. Don't get worked up. I'm coming round.

SARAH You don't come into this flat! You great stinking pig!

Everything you own! Everything you've touched! Out of the window!

DAVID (*attempting authority*) Now, Sarah!

SARAH Out in the street! Everything! Clothes! Scent! Books! Papers! Pyjama case!

DAVID Control yourself, Sarah. I'm coming round.

SARAH (*unheeding*) Briefcase! Travelling clock! Every little petty possession! And I'm leaving you!

(*But* DAVID *has already rushed out of the telephone box, leaving the phone dangling off the receiver rest.*)

SARAH You can live in your own squalor! I'm leaving you! David? David? The ignorant pig! (*And she flings the phone down in disgust. She picks up her coat and suitcase.*) I'm going. I'm going to Monica's.

VALERIE (*who has been enjoying the row, again finds herself personally involved*) Sarah, you can't go to Monica's!

(*But* SARAH *has swept out.*

DAVID *has entered the lobby and goes up in lift.*

STUART, *now wearing a raincoat and carrying a suitcase, has wandered on. He has the air of a man who has been through fire and water. Bracing back his shoulders, he enters the phone box decisively. He is puzzled to find the phone swinging from its hook. He picks it up.*)

STUART (*tentatively*) Hello? Hello? Hello?

(*Meanwhile* VALERIE *has crossed to pick up the discarded telephone in the living-room. She is about to replace the receiver when she hears the voice at the other end.*)

VALERIE Hello?

STUART Hello?

VALERIE Hello, David?

STUART My name is Stuart Wheeler.

VALERIE (*in surprise*) Stuart!

(*Upon which,* DAVID *bursts into the living-room. Although noting* VALERIE*'s presence, his first action is to rush across and open the bedroom door in search of* SARAH. VALERIE *watches him in trepidation.*)

STUART Valerie, I've got to see you.

VALERIE (*nervously*) Just a minute, Stuart. Something's cropped up.

(*During the above,* SARAH *has come out of the lift and*

crossed to "The Hussar." She hesitates for a moment and then goes in.

DAVID, *having ascertained that* SARAH *has gone out, now gives* VALERIE *his undivided attention. He strides ponderously towards her and surveys her, hands behind his back.*)

DAVID At last we meet. The cuckoo in the nest.

VALERIE (*timidly*) How do you do.

DAVID (*snarling*) Give me my telephone! (*He grabs it from her and speaks into it in tones of doom.*) This is David Lord speaking.

STUART (*with a gulp*) Sir, I am in love with your wife.

(DAVID *looks from the telephone to* VALERIE *with great cynicism and then back to the telephone, speaking with forced calm.*)

DAVID Now hear this. I know who you are. If you ever enter my premises again, sir, I shall put the police on you.

(*He puts the receiver down carefully. He turns to* VALERIE *and gives her a long, slow stare.*

STUART *puts down his telephone and, shaken by this encounter, leaves the telephone box. He picks up his suitcase, thinks for a moment, and walks into "The Hussar".*)

DAVID I don't think we've been introduced.

VALERIE I think we've spoken on the telephone.

DAVID That's very possible.

VALERIE I was just going.

DAVID Don't disturb yourself on my account. I'm only the sitting tenant.

VALERIE I'm sorry if we inconvenienced you.

DAVID And I suppose you and your paramour consider yourself sub-tenants. So when next you see him, you can tell him I'm drawing up a rental agreement retrospective and that the premium will be far and away beyond his meagre means.

VALERIE I doubt whether I will see him. I've no wish to see him.

DAVID That's your problem, madam. Anyway, you seem to be well acquainted with the domestic arrangements here. Perhaps you can tell me where I can find my wife.

VALERIE She's out at the moment. She said something about leaving you.

DAVID Was she—er—upset?

VALERIE (*diffidently*) Well——

DAVID I suppose you know all about our little contretemps?

VALERIE Vaguely.

DAVID Extraordinary imagination the woman has. She seems to have got hold of some wild idea that I'm still seeing that girl.

VALERIE Yes. (*She hands him the note from* MAXINE.)

DAVID Ah! And the funny thing is that there was no need for this missive at all—as the girl had already thanked me personally. Dated and signed. You know what it is? Subconsciously, she wants to break up my marriage.

VALERIE You were the one who kept the letter.

DAVID I know. Hell-bent on self-destruction. Another lemming plunging into the ocean of marital discontent. (*Pleased with the phrase, he begins to repeat it before a disturbing thought hits him.*) Another lemming plunging—— Did my wife say anything about coming back?

VALERIE No, she took a suitcase.

DAVID (*hoping for a negative answer*) You don't know where she's gone, I suppose?

VALERIE (*promptly*) Two hundred and thirty-eight Mount Street.

DAVID Ah! I'd better get round there.

VALERIE Yes.

DAVID Shortly.

VALERIE She'll be expecting you.

DAVID Yes, it's got to be faced.

VALERIE Yes.

DAVID Yes.

VALERIE She can't eat you.

(DAVID *has crossed to the drinks table and pours himself a stiff scotch.*)

DAVID I wish I could depend on that. (*He presses the soda syphon, which is empty.*) Blast!

VALERIE Oh, are we out of soda? I mean, are *you* out of soda? There's some little bottles on the shelf.

DAVID (*ironically*) Thank you.

VALERIE Bottle opener on the hook.

DAVID Thank you.

VALERIE The ice is in the——

DAVID Thank you! I am well acquainted with the geography of this flat, madam.

VALERIE Oh. Sorry.

DAVID Can I offer you a drink?

VALERIE No, thanks.

DAVID (*again ironical*) Don't hesitate to help yourself.

VALERIE Perhaps you feel that I owe you a word of explanation.

DAVID (*who has now poured himself a drink*) Oh, no, no, no, no! After all, it's not every day one finds an extra wife on the nominal roll. Come and go as you please. Liberty Hall. Invite a few friends in. Why not? Have a small party. Drink the gin—drink the scotch. Case of Portuguese Champagne in the wardrobe. Be my guest. Anything you can't find—just ask. Olives—cashew nuts—Alka-seltzer——

VALERIE It's in the bathroom cabinet.

DAVID I know where the Alka-seltzer is, madam! I don't spend *every* night of the week watching foreign films in Hampstead cinemas.

VALERIE I'm sorry about that. I wanted Sarah to take you to the Black and White Minstrel Show tonight. As a treat. But she wouldn't.

DAVID Did you really?

VALERIE I actually gave her the tickets.

DAVID How very thoughtful! How very kind. You're not at all what I imagined.

VALERIE What did you imagine?

DAVID Somebody—well—sultry.

VALERIE Oh, I am quite sultry.

DAVID Yes. I thought you must be. Weighing all the facts.

VALERIE (*archly*) Do you know all the facts?

DAVID Not quite. May I ask you a very personal question?

VALERIE All right.

DAVID Why did you pour West Indian Lime into my brief-case?

VALERIE I didn't. I wouldn't.

DAVID Somebody would. Somebody did. Last Friday.

VALERIE That would be Stuart. He's very jealous of you.

DAVID (*rather pleased*) Ah!

VALERIE I fear for his sanity sometimes.

DAVID A terrible thing, the green-eyed monster.

VALERIE He has the mind of a six-year-old child.

(*Over the above* DAVID *has noticed the jacket on the floor. He has picked it up and now surveys its sleeveless condition.*)

DAVID Yes. I know exactly what you mean.

VALERIE She got carried away. (*Pause.*) She only did it because she loves you. (*Pause.*) She got carried away.

(*There is then a long silence.* DAVID, *intrigued by the jacket, removes the jacket he is wearing and puts on the sleeveless one. He buttons it and looks first at one missing sleeve and then the other.*)

DAVID Yes, she ought to be carried away—in a straitjacket.

VALERIE She's done it to some other things too.

(DAVID *cannot really take this in for the moment. He is fascinated by the jacket.*)

DAVID The blue check?

VALERIE I think so.

DAVID The dog-tooth hacking jacket?

VALERIE Most things. (*Reassuringly.*) But only the sleeves. She hasn't touched a single trouser-leg.

DAVID What has she left me?

VALERIE (*brightening*) Oh, lots of things. All your sweaters.

DAVID (*with ironic cheerfulness*) Really? I've a Board Meeting of the British Travel Agents' Association tomorrow. I shall wear the canary-coloured pullover.

VALERIE You can't really blame her. You have behaved disgracefully.

DAVID I freely admit it. But how much can the human frame stand?

VALERIE You must go to her. Talk to her. Get her out of Mount Street.

DAVID Talk to her? Go to her? I'm not a complete fool. If she amputates my jackets what will she do to my person? No, I've a far better idea. I shall go to a night club.

VALERIE You can't.

DAVID I shall catch the early show, get stinking drunk and go on to another night club.

VALERIE But she loves you.

DAVID (*glancing at both sleeveless arms*) Obviously so. The woman's demented. She's no sense of proportion. Great heavens, I could have understood it if she'd gone off and had an affair herself. To even the score. I'd have accepted that quite calmly.

VALERIE But she did do.

DAVID She did what!

VALERIE By proxy.

DAVID Proxy?

VALERIE Through me. Isn't it obvious?

DAVID No.

VALERIE The only reason she let me come here, posing as your wife, was to get her own back on you. She took a vicarious pleasure out of imagining that your wife was sleeping with somebody else.

DAVID But *she's* my wife.

VALERIE Yes, that's the whole point.

DAVID H'm. Did you say vicarious?

VALERIE Pleasure. She was committing adultery by proxy. She was getting her own back on you. She was able to feel nice and promiscuous without actually—well, losing her honour.

DAVID H'm. (*Reflectively*.) Her mother's sister was rather a strange woman.

VALERIE You drove her to it, David.

DAVID Poor Sarah.

VALERIE You made her what she is.

DAVID Poor demented Sarah.

VALERIE Can't you imagine how she felt? Night after night. Sitting here. Knowing that you were making love to another woman.

DAVID But I didn't!

VALERIE Knowing that you—— You didn't what?

DAVID I didn't make love to her. I never slept with her.

VALERIE (*puzzled*) Maxine?

DAVID As God is my witness,. I never laid a finger on that girl. I wouldn't.

VALERIE You ought to be struck down dead.

DAVID It's true! It wasn't like that. She isn't like that. She's pure. She's innocent. She's wonderful.

VALERIE Is there something wrong with her?

DAVID No, madam, there is nothing wrong with her! And—I know what's in your mind!—there's nothing wrong with me either! What is it about you women? Why can you only put men into two categories? We're either sex maniacs or raving homosexuals. Aren't we allowed to enjoy a normal, worthwhile human relationship? Good grief, no wonder the world's going to the dogs. You can't even take girls to lunch these days without they assume you want to seduce them.

VALERIE But you do want to seduce them.

DAVID Yes, in God's good time. But we don't want *them* to seduce *us*. It's disgusting! You're halfway through your Vichyssoise, they've got one glass of Rosé inside them—and their long pink nails are scratching your knees under the table. Well, I was fortunate enough to find a girl who was different.

VALERIE But what did you *do* with her?

DAVID Talked. Chatted.

VALERIE No, I mean physically?

DAVID (*with great dignity*) We held hands.

VALERIE Is that all? Ever?

DAVID A chaste kiss as one helped her into a cab.

VALERIE And you haven't told Sarah?

DAVID No.

VALERIE In heaven's name why not?

DAVID She wouldn't understand. She'd laugh at me.

VALERIE No! (*She tries to keep a straight face but fails. She speaks with a giggle.*) Why should she—— (*She has to break off. Now she is shrieking with laughter. Finally she manages to gasp out.*) Why should she laugh at you?

DAVID (*stares at her coldly*) Quite.

VALERIE (*composing herself*) I'm sorry. (*Making a great effort to keep a straight face.*) There. Go on.

DAVID Go on where?

VALERIE Tell me why you couldn't make love to her.

DAVID I didn't say I couldn't. I said I didn't.

VALERIE Don't you mean you haven't—yet?

DAVID There's no yet about it, madam. Our relationship is a closed book with effect from tonight. I was talking to a chap only this evening—very shrewd fellow—he put me clear on a few points. I am ruining that girl's life. (*During this he has picked up the telephone and dialled telegrams. To the operator:*) Ah! This is Kensington 2902, I want to send a telegram, please. To Miss Maxine Scott-Whitney. Care of The Crescent Garage, Cromwell Road Extension. Message reads: Darling regret unable continue relationship with effect from tonight all love Squirrel Nutkin. (*Brusquely, aside to* VALERIE.) That's—er—a name that she has for me. (*Back into the telephone.*) No, Sir, it is not a greetings telegram. Thank you.

(*He puts down the telephone and paces the room as he talks.* VALERIE, *although apparently listening seriously, takes the opportunity while his back is turned of shoving a handkerchief in her mouth to prevent herself from laughing.*)

DAVID Yes, Maxine Scott-Whitney is an eighteen-year-old child and barely out of convent school. She knows the world—Cannes, Kitzbuehl, Majorca—but she knows little of worldly ways. It was not for me to—as it were—cast the first stone. (*He has now come face to face with* VALERIE *again. She is gazing at him seriously but with the handkerchief still stuffed in her mouth.*) But I see I am wasting my time.

VALERIE (*has snatched the handkerchief away*) Not at all, David. She sounds wonderful.

DAVID (*aggressively*) She is wonderful.

VALERIE But you must tell Sarah.

DAVID What—that she's a sweet innocent——?

VALERIE No, you fool! That you didn't sleep with her!

DAVID (*thinks about this*) Do you think she'd understand?

VALERIE She doesn't have to understand. She just has to know!

DAVID She'd laugh. It was a simple, pure love. She'd make a mockery of it.

VALERIE But David, you don't understand! She's in a terrible state. You're dealing with a woman. She might do anything. She might go round to Maxine's. With a pair of scissors. Cut off her hair—cut up her clothes—anything!

DAVID She wouldn't do that. (*He looks at his own sleeves and has second thoughts.*) She doesn't know where Maxine lives.

VALERIE Isn't she in the phone book?

DAVID Oh, God! (*He suddenly propels himself towards the door.*)

VALERIE David!

(VALERIE *calls after him as he moves out of the flat.*)

Sleeves, David!

(*The lift descends. During the above,* SARAH *has emerged from "The Hussar" with her suitcase. Now* STUART *also emerges from "The Hussar" with his suitcase and eyes her speculatively. Pause, and then the lift ascends again.*)

STUART Quite pleasant if the rain keeps off.

SARAH Yes.

(VALERIE *picks up* DAVID*'s glass and moves into the bedroom.* DAVID *dashes into the flat and changes his sleeveless jacket for the one he was wearing earlier.*)

VALERIE (*at the bedroom door*) Two hundred and thirty-eight Mount Street!

(DAVID *dashes out.*)

STUART (*diffidently*) I wonder if I—er—can get you a drink at all?

SARAH (*starchily*) I'll get my own drink, thank you.

(*She goes into "The Hussar".* DAVID *comes galloping down the stairs. He crosses past "The Hussar" where he sees* STUART.)

STUART (*cheerily*) 'Evening again!

DAVID Ah! 'Evening again! How did it go for you?

STUART Terrible. How did it go for you?

DAVID Terrible. Ah, well, press on.

(*They nod amiably and* DAVID *moves off.* SARAH *comes out of "The Hussar" carrying a drink. She sits down again. There is a long silence during which* STUART *flashes* SARAH *a couple of sidelong glances. He clears his throat.*)

STUART (*to himself*) Yes. Quite pleasant. (*He examines his glass, studiously not looking at* SARAH.) Great Scott! (*A quick glance from* SARAH *and he is encouraged to continue.*) Great zonking chip the size of a threepenny bit out of this glass! Ought to complain really. Still, always drink on the other side. No harm done. Cheers!
(SARAH *gives him a polite little smile.*)
Pleasant little pub. Of course, Sunday morning's the time. Actors, guardsmen, that calibre. Show biz.

SARAH Yes.

STUART Yes. Yes. (*He clears his throat again.*) By the way, I hope you didn't think I was being presumptuous.

SARAH What?

STUART In offering to top you up.
(*She looks at him, not understanding.*)
Drinkwise. No ulterior motive. One feels that this is the kind of pub where one can top them up for any Tom, Dick or Harry. Not that I class you with any Tom, Dick or Harry.

SARAH (*smiling*) Thank you.

STUART What I mean is, I wasn't trying to pick you up.

SARAH Weren't you?

STUART Not in this instance. I've got enough on my plate, thank you very much. (*Tapping his suitcase.*) Worldly possessions. (*Again rapping his suitcase.*) Goods and chattels. (*With a nod at her suitcase, abruptly changing the subject.*) That's rather smart. Are those fibre-glass jobs all they're cracked up to be?

SARAH The small ones are too small and the big ones are full of coat-hangers.

STUART That's one of the small ones, of course.

SARAH It's all I could carry. I shall send round for the big one tomorrow.

STUART (*realising that she, too, has left home*) Don't say we're both in the same boat?

SARAH I'd rather not talk about it. After all, when one has been married to an adulterous sex maniac, what is there to say?

STUART H'm. (*A tactful pause.*) I'm a canvas grip man myself.

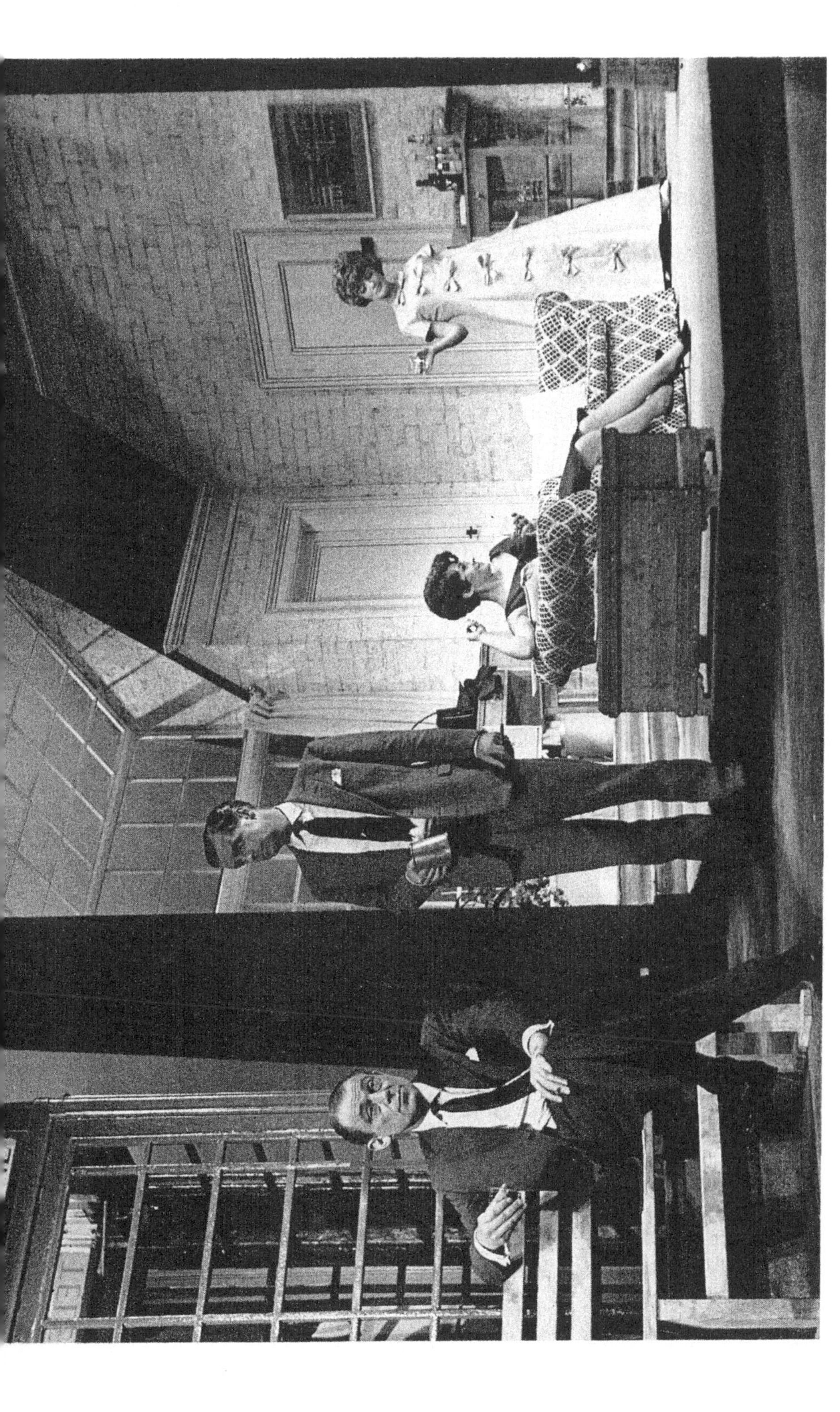

Yes, a large canvas grip—went right through the Air Force with me. I shall send round for that tomorrow.

SARAH I shall send for everything I possess.

STUART So shall I. (*Reflecting.*) Just on a point of order—whom *does* one send on these occasions?

SARAH I don't know. I've never done it before. I think when it comes down to it you have to go yourself.

STUART Oh, well, I shall just abandon everything then. I'm not going through that again. (*Brightening.*) New start, new life. All round to Simpson's in the morning. Couple of shirts, tie, socks, suit and a pair of pyjamas. That should keep me going. Nail-scissors. Tell me, without wishing to pry, what was your decision about the toothpaste?

SARAH Toothpaste?

STUART Yes. Did you pack it or leave it behind?

SARAH I packed it. Naturally.

STUART That's interesting. I took the view that toothpaste belongs to the surviving partner. Household effects.

SARAH (*rather sadly*) I took the view that I was the surviving partner.

STUART As indeed you are. Yes! The survival of the fittest! How long have you been married?

SARAH (*still sadly*) Seven years.

STUART (*proudly*) Nine!

(*Pause.*)

SARAH How do you feel?

STUART Marvellous! How do you feel?

SARAH (*in a small voice*) Marvellous.

STUART What's wrong?

SARAH Nothing. (*Pause, wistfully.*) Just think, I shall never throw another glass of scotch in his face, as long as I live. I miss him. I want him.

STUART After all he must have done to you?

SARAH After all I've done to him. He'll never forgive me. (*Looks at her watch.*) It's seventeen minutes since I left home and he hasn't been to look for me.

STUART (*nodding sagely*) He'll be in a night club.

SARAH Already?

STUART Oh, yes. Coat on—straight out—"Taxi!" Catch the early show. Then off to another night club. For the late show.

SARAH How callous.

STUART He's the deserted husband figure. It's expected of him. Arms round a couple of hostesses. Bottle of champagne. Box of Benson & Hedges and a Teddy bear. Blind raving drunk so the whole world can point at him and say, "My God, he's suffering!"

SARAH And what about the deserted wife figure? Just let her go into a restaurant alone and try to order one dry martini before dinner and a sort of low pitched buzz goes round the place from the waiters upwards: "Look at her—on the game already."

STUART I'd invite you out to dinner, on a friendly basis of course, if I didn't have my hands full.

SARAH You're very kind.

STUART Yes, it's the night of the long knives for me. Operation Co-respondent. Girl I'm involved with, married, you see. Got to have a showdown with the husband.

SARAH What are you going to say to him?

STUART I've a great deal to say—if only I can persuade him to listen. Trouble is, you try to talk to the chap—he just gets insulting, aggressive—hangs up.

SARAH Perhaps he's distraught. Perhaps he loves his wife.

STUART Nothing of the kind! The man's got a mistress! He's an adulterer, a liar, he's mean, furtive—leaves his wife at home while he gallivants round the best London restaurants with some little floozie he's picked up. What can you say to a man like that?

SARAH (*automatically*) You foul, filthy, dirty, adulterous pig.

STUART That's rather good.

SARAH I've had the practice.

STUART "You foul, filthy——" That rings rather a bell with me.

SARAH Perhaps your wife called you it. It's a woman's line.

STUART Unfortunately. He wouldn't take it from me, man to man.

SARAH (*gulps back her drink*) I'd call him it.

STUART (*smiles slyly*) Would you really?

SARAH Why not? They're all the same. I'd like to go round London with a loudspeaker van, addressing the whole male population. "You foul, filthy, dirty, adulterous pigs".

STUART I'd like to see his face when you said it.

SARAH (*rises*) I'll do it. Do you want me to?

STUART (*thinks for a moment*) What have we got to lose?

SARAH I'll ring him up and tell him what he is.

STUART Then I'll take over. I'll say, "You've heard what you are, sir, from an independent witness. Now hear this. I am in love with your wife".

(*They cross to the telephone box.* SARAH *opens the door and picks up the telephone. She holds the door ajar, half in and half out of the telephone box.*)

SARAH What's the number?

STUART (*fumbling in his pockets*) It's Kensington—— Oh, just a minute—threepenny bits.

(*He nips into "The Hussar".* DAVID *enters, is about to pass the telephone box on his way home, and sees* SARAH.)

DAVID Sarah!

SARAH David!

DAVID I've been going frantic. I've been to Mount Street—you weren't there—I thought you were in the river.

SARAH I thought you were in a night club.

DAVID At a time like this? Look, darling, I know I've been a brute and a swine, but—(*Suddenly puzzled by the telephone.*) What are you doing in there?

SARAH (*thinking quickly*) I was ringing you up. At a night club.

DAVID I don't need night clubs, or other women. I need you, Sarah. Won't you at least come home and talk about it?

(SARAH *has come out of the telephone box and picks up her suitcase which* DAVID *takes from her.*)

SARAH (*thinks for a moment*) But you're still seeing her.

DAVID If I'm still seeing her why am I chasing around after you?

SARAH You have a lot of explaining to do.

DAVID (*with romantic pomposity*) There comes a time in every marriage when the need is for actions—not explanations.

(*He takes her arm purposefully and leads her over to the lobby.*)

SARAH I cut off all your sleeves.

DAVID I know. And I love you for it.

(*He puts his arm around her and they enter the lift.* STUART *comes out of "The Hussar", opens the telephone box door and is surprised to find the box empty. He looks around, and then enters the box himself. He picks up the telephone and pauses before dialling, rehearsing what he is going to say.*

During the above VALERIE *has come out of the bedroom and walks out of the flat. As* DAVID *and* SARAH *enter the flat,* VALERIE *comes down the stairs into the lobby, crosses and sits on the bench outside "The Hussar".*

DAVID *and* SARAH *pause at the door and kiss.*)

SARAH Explanations?

DAVID (*firmly*) Actions.

(*He leads her towards the bedroom.* STUART *has now dialled and the telephone in the living-room rings.*)

DAVID (*impatiently*) Oh!

(SARAH *crosses to answer the telephone.* DAVID *crosses with her and puts his arm round her as she lifts the receiver.*)

SARAH Yes?

(*We hear the pay pips and* STUART *puts in a coin.*)

STUART Put your husband on the line.

(SARAH, *mildly surprised by the rudeness, hands the receiver to* DAVID.)

SARAH Don't be long, darling.

(DAVID *looks after her lecherously as she goes into the bedroom and closes the door behind her. He turns to the telephone.*)

DAVID (*genially*) David Lord speaking.

STUART Sir, you are a foul, filthy, dirty, adulterous pig!

DAVID (*with tired impatience*) Now look here, old chap. Don't you think it's time you called it a day? You're the victim of a great misunderstanding and I pity you.

STUART Sir, I am in love with your wife.

DAVID My dear good fellow, you are not in love with my wife. Furthermore, my wife is not in love with you. My wife happens to be passionately in love with me. And we both fervently hope that you will never trouble us again. I wish you a civil goodnight.

(DAVID *puts down the telephone and rubbing his hands, trots into the bedroom.*

STUART, *stunned, replaces the receiver. He steps out of the phone box and is surprised to see* VALERIE *sitting outside the pub.*)

VALERIE It's no good, Stuart. I don't want to talk to you.

STUART I know. I've just spoken to your husband. I hope you'll both be very happy.

VALERIE You didn't ring David!

STUART We exchanged a few words. Obviously the man's got some kind of fatal hold over you. Some—sexual hypnosis, I imagine.

VALERIE Don't be so ridiculous.

STUART Very well. (*Picking up his suitcase.*) You're passionately in love with him—he's passionately in love with you. Exit seemingly undersexed third party, carrying suitcase. I'd just like to mention that I left my wife tonight on your account.

VALERIE (*with sympathetic exasperation*) Oh, Stuart! You didn't!

STUART I shall manage. I've served my purpose in your life. I'm only glad that the woman I love has found true happiness. Even if it is on a purely erotic level. I don't blame you—I blame myself. You quarrel with me. I leave you in a—— (*Delicately.*) over-excited state. Husband comes in. Obviously you can't keep your hands off him. (*Incredulously.*) What does he do—give you drugs? Or have you just decided to abandon yourself to a life of complete erotic——

(VALERIE *has picked up a drink which has been left on the bench. She throws it in his face.* STUART *resignedly puts his suitcase on the bench and opens it. He fishes out a hand-towel labelled* HIS *and mops his face meticulously. He folds the towel neatly and replaces it in the suitcase. He puts the suitcase on the ground and crosses to the telephone box. He takes two directories from the telephone box and returns to the bench where he sits down.*)

STUART Bayswater, that's the area. Small hotel tonight. Somewhere to lay my head. (*He has opened one of the directories and is running a finger down it.*) Tomorrow morning I shall tramp the streets for a small furnished room, suitable for a man who is picking up the threads of a shattered life.

VALERIE (*coldly*) Try the Holland Gardens Hotel. It's in Holland Gardens.

STUART I shall find my own hotel, thank you very much.

(*He browses through the telephone directories.* VALERIE *disregards him.*

In the flat the bedroom door is flung open and DAVID, *in shirtsleeves, bursts into the living-room.*)

DAVID I can't do it!

(SARAH, *wearing the familiar housecoat, follows him into the living-room.*)

SARAH David!

DAVID It's futile, Sarah. Our marriage is in ruins. We've got nothing in common. What can we solve by going to bed? It's a complete shambles from beginning to end.

SARAH It's not a shambles.

DAVID It's a shambles, woman! Go in there! Look at it! Shambles! Sleeves all over the floor!

SARAH You can have a new suit.

DAVID Bathroom! Complete chaos! Broken bottles! Whole place stinking of West Indian Lime!

SARAH I'll buy you some more.

DAVID What's the point? You're not stable, Sarah. We haven't got the basis of a stable marriage.

SARAH There were faults on both sides, David.

DAVID This goes deeper than faults.

SARAH In fact rather more on your side than on mine. If you want to analyse our marriage——

DAVID (*in alarm*) Now I didn't say that!

SARAH If it's a question of sitting down, quietly, and working out, step by step——

DAVID (*hastily*) I've told you I love you. I can't say more than that.

SARAH It's not what people say in marriage—it's what they do.

DAVID (*crossing to her*) Now, darling——

SARAH It's what they've done.

DAVID (*urgently*) I love you, Sarah!

(SARAH *is about to speak but* DAVID, *to shut her up, hastily kisses her. After a moment she responds.*)

DAVID Come on!

(They move briskly into the bedroom and the door closes behind them.

Outside "The Hussar", STUART *finally locates an address in the telephone directory.)*

STUART Ah! This looks a possible. Holland Gardens Hotel. Holland Gardens.

VALERIE Thirty-one bus.

STUART *(rises)* I wouldn't insult you by going out of your life in anything less than a taxi. *(He picks up the suitcase and braces himself as if to move off.)* Goodbye, Valerie.

VALERIE Goodbye, Stuart.

STUART *(reluctant to go)* Yes, I shall miss this area. South Ken. The pub. The flat. You.

VALERIE What are you going to do?

STUART I'm going to pick up the threads of my——

VALERIE Yes, I know. I mean when you've picked them up.

STUART Who knows? I shan't brood, I can assure you of that. I shall find somebody, no doubt—given time. Not a grand passion. Possibly a showgirl—I believe they're quite warmhearted.

VALERIE It's what you need, Stuart. Someone kind and understanding.

STUART *(with asperity)* Someone single—that's the prime consideration. Anyway, you'll be all right. With him. You'll lead a pretty full life.

VALERIE *(sadly)* Will I?

STUART *(bitterly)* Yes. I expect I shall think of you often—leading it.

(With this horrible thought, he rises abruptly and again takes up his suitcase.)

STUART *(dramatically)* Valerie. You've always been honest with me.

VALERIE I've tried to be.

STUART It's the one thing I've valued above all else. You were nothing if not frank and forthright. Before I go I want to ask you one thing. Were you really in love with me?

VALERIE I was really in love with you.

STUART Thank you. *(He turns to go.)*

VALERIE Stuart! (*He turns back.*) Won't I ever see you again?

STUART I doubt it.

VALERIE We could meet, if you wanted to. When you've got your own flat. Don't you see—it would be even easier? I could come and see you. Friday nights. I could say I was going to see a foreign film.

STUART It's not enough, Valerie.

VALERIE Wednesdays and Fridays, even. Twice a week.

STUART I should want more than that.

VALERIE Mondays, Wednesdays and Fridays?

STUART (*putting down his suitcase*) You don't understand, Valerie. We wouldn't be happy. I've been giving it some thought tonight—happiness. Do you know what true happiness is? I'll tell you. It's——

VALERIE It's love, Stuart.

STUART Yes, but it's more than that. It's being out together. Being seen by other people. Walking down Coventry Street—holding hands. Meeting each other's friends. Example: chap I was having a drink with tonight. On this very bench. Friendly type. Wouldn't mind meeting him again. You see, I could never introduce you to that man.

VALERIE But we could have all that! I'll walk down Coventry Street if that's what you want.

STUART It's no use. I'm a jealous man. Whatever we did, where-ever we went—you'd always be going back, every night, to him.

VALERIE Stuart—supposing I did leave David?

STUART (*a double-take*) Supposing what?

VALERIE I'll leave him. Now. I won't even bother to collect my things.

STUART (*astounded*) But you're passionately in love with him.

VALERIE I never said so.

STUART You'll leave him?

VALERIE I've left him.

(*He stares at her for a moment incredulously. He takes her in his arms. They kiss.*)

STUART I love you, Valerie.

VALERIE I love you, Stuart.

STUART We'll find a flat. Tomorrow. Together,

VALERIE No, Stuart.

STUART We'll stay at the Holland Gardens Hotel tonight, then in the morning——

VALERIE No, Stuart!

(Pause. He looks at her.)

I'm not going to live with you.

STUART But you said——

VALERIE I said I was going to leave my husband. But I can't live with you!

STUART Woman! The immortal sphut— slinx! In heaven's name, why not?

VALERIE *(floundering for an excuse)* It's—it's so old-fashioned, Stuart. "Living in sin". I've known people who tried it. Rooms in Earls Court. Gas-rings. Sharing bathrooms with liberal-minded art students. And they look at you liberally when you pass them on the stairs. It wouldn't work, Stuart.

STUART But it won't be like that. Not for long. We'd get married as soon as we could.

VALERIE *(glumly)* Yes, I know.

STUART And then it'll be marvellous! Just think of it! *(Lyrically.)* Married! Evenings out, evenings at home. Breakfasts. Togetherness. Toothbrushes nestling side by side.

(VALERIE *has screwed up her face into an expression of excruciating pain. She can stand it no longer.*)

VALERIE Stop it, Stuart!

STUART *(surprised)* But that's what we want, isn't it?

VALERIE *(thinking quickly)* If I come and live with you now, he'll never divorce me.

STUART Rubbish!

VALERIE He'd refuse me a divorce out of spite.

STUART *(judiciously)* Mmmm. Yes. That makes sense.

VALERIE We can still see each other. I'll come round to you. Mondays, Wednesdays and Fridays.

STUART And then he'll give you a divorce?

VALERIE He's bound to. Eventually.

STUART But how will you live? Where will you go? What will you do?

VALERIE I've got a friend in Mount Street. Her husband's in this submarine. She'd take me in. Then I thought I might find a job.

STUART (*a masculine smile*) Doing what?

VALERIE I don't know. I thought I might become an analytical chemist.

STUART (*he laughs indulgently*) Yes, well. Still that's no problem. There's agencies; light secretarial work; receptionist—Mondays, Wednesdays——

VALERIE And Fridays.

STUART Sundays?

VALERIE (*doubtfully*) Well—perhaps. Some Sundays. We can't overdo it in case he has me followed.

STUART Point taken. (*Considers for a moment.*) All right. O.K. We're in business.

VALERIE Do we shake hands?

STUART We'll have a drink on it.

VALERIE (*as they move into "The Hussar"*) I thought perhaps every third Sunday——

(*As they disappear into "The Hussar", the bedroom door in the flat is again flung open. This time it is* SARAH *who bounds out, followed by* DAVID.)

SARAH I can't do it!

DAVID Sarah!

SARAH I'm sorry, darling, I just find the whole idea completely revolting.

DAVID I always thought we were well-adjusted as far as the physical side was concerned. If you're going to crack up on that front, what have we got left?

SARAH (*bitterly*) Nothing, David. We haven't got anything.

DAVID It's all right, darling. I can be understanding. With patience and tolerance we can sort it out.

SARAH You sound like Eustace Chesser.

DAVID You're overwrought.

SARAH Of course I'm overwrought! Three months of apologies and "Oh, darling, forgive me, forgive me!" I thought in all our married life we'd never been as close.

DAVID Close! It's just been one row after another!

SARAH Rows, yes. But after the rows—— (*Pause.*) And all the time you were still seeing that girl and you were just as close with her. I'm sorry, David, I'm not entirely without feelings.

DAVID (*formally*) Sarah. Would you sit down? There's something I want to tell you.

SARAH I don't want to hear any more.

DAVID Please, Sarah. This is important.

(*She sits down reluctantly.* DAVID *picks his words carefully.*)

I should have told you this before. The only reason I haven't told you is because I've been a complete coward. I thought you would laugh at me. There's nothing a man fears so much as ridicule.

SARAH What do you want to tell me?

DAVID I don't care if you do laugh at me. I want to set your mind at rest. I never took Maxine to bed.

SARAH (*quietly*) What?

DAVID And that's the truth. Can you believe that?

SARAH (*thinks for a moment*) Yes. I can believe that?

DAVID And you don't think it's funny?

SARAH (*in a tired voice*) No, I don't think it's funny, David. (*She sits back in her chair as if exhausted.*) Could I have a drink, please?

(DAVID, *registering relief, crosses and pours her a drink.*)

DAVID Stiff one?

SARAH Fine.

(*He brings her back the drink and hands it to her solicitously.* SARAH *takes it and tosses it into his face.*)

SARAH (*leaping to her feet*) You didn't sleep with her! How dare you! All these months of deceit and it wasn't even sex! How dare you!

DAVID (*plaintively*) I thought you'd be pleased.

SARAH Pleased! You've made a fool of me!

DAVID I haven't made a fool of you!

SARAH If you'd slept with her you'd have made a fool of nobody but yourself. But this! Loping about London with your mouth half-open, gazing into the face of that squint-eyed bitch. That makes a fool of *me*!

DAVID I thought you'd be relieved.

SARAH Relieved! Because you're stupid enough to pick up that cheap little trollop—and you don't even sleep with her! What was she for? Month after month after month after month you're out with her, feeding her, pouring drink into her, lighting her cigarettes, standing up when she comes back from the loo. Idolising her! Talking to her! Sitting with her! Being with her! And why? Because you preferred her bloody company! All right! (*She storms into the bedroom.*)

DAVID Sarah! No! Sarah!

(*He rushes after her. The bedroom door closes behind them.*

STUART, *followed by* VALERIE, *rushes out of "The Hussar". He is still carrying the suitcase.*)

STUART No, I'm sorry, Valerie. He's got to divorce you.

VALERIE Stuart, you'll spoil everything.

STUART (*plonking the suitcase down by the bench*) It's no use arguing. I'm going to see him now.

VALERIE (*desperately*) He's gone out.

(*But* STUART *has already picked up his suitcase and moved off.* VALERIE *rushes into the telephone box and hastily dials.* STUART *has reached the lobby and goes up the stairs. The phone in the living-room rings. We hear sounds of an angry argument in the bedroom.*)

DAVID (*off*) You're trying to drive me out of my mind.

SARAH (*off*) Yes!

(*The bedroom door is flung open and* DAVID *storms into the living-room. He is carrying a pair of trousers of which one leg has been hacked off.*)

DAVID Good grief, woman! I seriously think you need medical attention!

(*He flings the trousers down and picks up the telephone as* SARAH *follows him into the room. She is now wearing her coat again.*)

DAVID (*angrily*) David Lord speaking!

(*We hear the pay pips and* VALERIE *pushes in a coin.*)

VALERIE (*hastily*) David, I must speak to Sarah. It's very urgent.

(*Upon which the door is dramatically flung open and* STUART *enters the room.* DAVID *has turned impatiently to* SARAH *and sees* STUART *with surprise.*)

STUART Sir, I am in love with your wife!

SARAH (*faintly*) But we've only just met.

DAVID (*into telephone*) Do you think you could possibly ring back? Something's cropped up.

(*And he rings off. During the following* VALERIE *comes out of the telephone box, offers a silent prayer to heaven, and goes back into "The Hussar".*)

STUART (*to* DAVID) Sorry, old chap. (*Looking around the room.*) Am I in the right flat? Yes. Right flat—wrong chap. Boobed. (*Looking from* DAVID *to* SARAH.) Do you two know each other?

DAVID Vaguely. (*To* SARAH, *accusingly.*) You two apparently do.

SARAH We met for five minutes. We had something in common. He'd left his wife—I'd left my husband.

STUART (*cheerfully*) So basically, we're all on the loose together.

DAVID Some of us may be on the loose—others not. I don't know whether you've had a couple too many, but this lady happens to be my wife.

STUART Great Scott! (*To* SARAH.) Together again, eh? (*To* DAVID.) Congratulations. Hope I didn't let the cat out of the bag.

DAVID What do you want?

STUART I've come to see the master of the house. David Lord. Presumably you're friends of his.

DAVID Is your name Stuart?

STUART Yes.

SARAH Oh, my God.

DAVID I'm David Lord.

STUART Oh, my God. (*Puzzled.*) But that's not Valerie.

DAVID That's Sarah.

SARAH I'm his wife.

STUART (*to* DAVID) You bigamist!

DAVID (*rounding on* SARAH) There you are! Oh what a tangled web we weave! All right—tell him! (*To* STUART.) I believe you owe me four pounds. West Indian Lime. I'll have that now. (*To* SARAH.) Go on—tell him!

SARAH You see, he's not actually married to Valerie.

DAVID There's also the question of my whisky, consumed on these premises.

SARAH He's actually married to me.

DAVID We'll call that two pounds. (*Suddenly raising his voice.*) Well, don't stand there with your mouth open, man! Get your wallet out! Poppy up!

STUART (*bewildered*) You're David Lord?

DAVID Yes! I'd prefer cash, but I'll accept a cheque.

(STUART *picks up the framed photograph of* SARAH.)

STUART And you're Mrs. David Lord. But then who——?

SARAH She was pretending to be me. She didn't want to get involved.

DAVID (*to* STUART) It's no use staring at that! If you stare at it all night it's still my wife! You've been taken for a ride, laddie!

SARAH Don't be so nasty, David!

DAVID Don't *you* start! I sat through a whole season of Eisenstein at the National Film Theatre on that clown's behalf. The man's a buffoon! He's gullible! He'd swallow anything.

SARAH He's not as gullible as you! At least he slept with the girl!

STUART (*who has been in a daze*) And she *isn't* Mrs. David Lord! Who is she then?

DAVID She's a single girl! She lives in a flat with five other single girls! Single!

STUART I trusted that woman.

SARAH At least she was a woman. She wasn't a cheap little, silly little, spotty adolescent.

DAVID Maxine is not spotty!

SARAH A little, mimsy, celibate slut!

DAVID We'll not have this argument in front of strangers!

SARAH I'll have this argument where and when I bloody well like!

DAVID You will not!

SARAH I'm not going to argue with you—I'm going out.

DAVID Go out! Stay out! Take your suitcase!

SARAH I wouldn't give you the satisfaction! (*She goes out, slamming the door behind her. During the following she comes down in the lift and goes into "The Hussar".*)

DAVID (*shouting after her*) Don't bother to come back. (*He wheels on* STUART.) I blame you for all this.

STUART (*surprised*) All what?

DAVID My broken marriage. I lay it exclusively at your door.

STUART Steady on. Haven't I got enough problems of my own without shouldering yours? Anyway, you told me yourself that you were in love with this other girl.

DAVID Exactly. And for why? I'd have finished with the girl three months ago if it hadn't been for you. I'd have got over it by now. (*Noting that* STUART *is still clutching the photograph of* SARAH.) Do you mind? (*He snatches the photograph from* STUART.) Three months! Every Friday. Satisfying the cultural requirements of my wife while you were satisfying—well, I don't know—whatever the woman's requirements were.

STUART Rather poor taste, that remark.

DAVID Is it? Three months! How would you like it? Week after week of foreign hogwash.

STUART It was only one night a week.

DAVID It wasn't only one night a week. Saturdays and Sundays —the big debate. "What did you think of the Odessa Steps sequence in Potemkin?" "I don't know, I was asleep". "Yes, you're a moron. Why don't you go and watch the cowboys and indians with Maxine?" Is it any wonder that I did?

STUART I see your point.

DAVID I'm glad somebody does.

STUART I can only assure you that had I known the circumstances three months ago I would never have set foot in your home.

DAVID (*mollified*) Well, I suppose we all make tragic mistakes at one time or another.

STUART (*taking out his wallet*) I believe you said six pounds—including the scotch.

DAVID We won't fret about that.

STUART No, I insist. I only drank your scotch under the impression that I was committing adultery with your wife. Had I known that I was committing it with somebody else—I would have brought my own.

DAVID (*as* STUART *offers him the money*) No. Really.

STUART I wish you would.

DAVID All right. I'll tell you what. Give me four quid for the aftershave and we'll call it a day.

(STUART *hands him four pounds.*)

Ta! So much for sordid business. Do sit down.

(STUART *does so.*)

No, it's a pity we didn't meet earlier. We might have saved each other a great deal of bother.

STUART (*feelingly*) Yes. A great deal of bother.

DAVID You—er—left the wife then?

STUART Had to.

DAVID Smooth exit, was it?

STUART No.

DAVID Oh dear me. Trouble? Recriminations?

(STUART *nods glumly.*)

Yes. Wives are like that. What did she say?

STUART (*rising*) It wasn't so much what she said——

(*He peels off his raincoat, revealing that like* DAVID *before him, he is wearing a jacket whose sleeves have been hacked off above the elbows.* DAVID'*s heart goes out to him and he grasps* STUART'*s upper arm in silent sympathy. he crosses and pours two drinks.* STUART *takes out his wallet.*)

DAVID This one's on the house.

(SARAH *and* VALERIE *walk out of "The Hussar" together, carrying drinks, and sit on the bench.*

Meanwhile DAVID *has crossed and handed* STUART *his drink. All four sit nursing their drinks and brooding for a moment.*)

STUART Women! I don't understand them.

(STUART *and* DAVID *relax with their drinks, both lost in their own ruminations.*)

VALERIE I just don't understand men. Was Stuart very annoyed?

SARAH I suppose he feels cheated.

VALERIE Supposing I'd said at the very beginning, "I'm a single girl", and I'd behaved like every woman who's the other woman. If I'd made his life hell, nagged him, pestered him at his office, made scenes, he'd have been ill and harassed, but he'd have loved me for it.

SARAH Well, I give up. I thought I had the ideal marriage. I've tried to be the perfect wife. I've been an absolute bitch. We've had rows, recriminations, screaming matches. I've put colour into our marriage, but it was all a fraud, a shame and all those marvellous rows have been for nothing.

STUART I feel so ruddy cheated, that's the thing. If only she'd said "I'm a single girl, and I don't want to get married" then I could have behaved like every other husband with a bit on the side. "Look duckie, we've had a few giggles, but I've got a wife to consider". I could have dropped her like a red-hot brick, and she'd have been potty about me. They don't want us to behave honourably.

DAVID Don't talk to me about honourable behaviour. Look at me. I could have been the biggest cad of the lot, had I so wished. Into bed, out of bed. Different little dolly girl every night of the week. There'd have been rows, but basically she'd have admired me for it. And she could have boasted about it. You know—"He always comes back to me"—that bit.

SARAH Still, he's not so bad as husbands go.

VALERIE I wonder if Stuart's cooled off yet. After all, he is in love with me.

DAVID No, I've got to go on living with the woman. I have got responsibilities, after all.

STUART I've burned my boats. It's Valerie or nobody. I shall just have to come to some arrangement with the girl.

SARAH Let's go and find them.

VALERIE We've got to.

STUART Shall we go and find them?

DAVID We've got to.

SARAH Come on.

DAVID I tell you what. (*Pause.*) I thought I might pop into a night club first.

STUART That's a very good idea.

(SARAH *and* VALERIE *cross into the lobby and enter the lift.*)

DAVID (*slipping on his one intact jacket*) We'll catch the early show. We might pop on to somewhere else for the late show.

STUART You couldn't lend me a jacket, I suppose?

DAVID Er—— (*He decides not to confess.*) oh, they lend you jackets in these places.

(STUART *picks up his raincoat and suitcase and they go out.*

The stage is empty for some moments before the door of the living-room is flung open again and VALERIE, SARAH, DAVID *and* STUART *sweep in, arguing and gesticulating and all talking at once.*)

STUART (*to* VALERIE) Of all the mean, shabby, hypocritical, underhanded schemes I've ever heard of—— You're just a compulsive liar. It's an obsession. What you need is medical attention——

SARAH (*to* DAVID) It's a Lolita complex—that's what it is with you. You ought to be locked up. Put away. It's Freudian. Sick. You're not safe to be let loose on the streets——

VALERIE (*to* STUART) You have the mind of a child! A fifteen-year-old boy. You're like a schoolgirl, dreaming about thatched cottages. Well, life isn't like that, Stuart! You've got to grow up——

DAVID (*to* SARAH) Heavens above, woman, it was harmless! Harmless! All right, I took her to lunch—I was extravagant—I've admitted it! But for crying out loud, are you going to go on and on and on and on and on——

STUART (*to* SARAH) Don't you agree? Don't you think the best thing for all concerned would be if she went and saw a psychiatrist——

SARAH (*to* STUART) I'm not making a thing of this, am I? Can't you see my point? Am I being unreasonable? He's not healthy, chasing young girls like that——

VALERIE (*to* DAVID) I'm right, aren't I? Can't you explain to that—mental teenager! That there's more to life than roses rambling round the door——

DAVID (*to* VALERIE) You're a friend of hers. Can't you get through to her? And point out what she's doing? Going on and on and on and on and on and on——

STUART (*back to* VALERIE) She agrees with me! It's the general concensus of opinion that you're off your flaming rocker! You're twisted! Warped! You're off your head——

SARAH (*back to* DAVID) Ask him! That's all you've got to do! He'll tell you! I could understand adultery! I could understand you falling for a woman! But ogling at school-children! It's ludicrous! It's retarded!

VALERIE (*back to* STUART) There you are! And that's a male opinion! That's not my opinion! It's his opinion! For God's sake grow up, Stuart! Make the effort! Mature!

DAVID (*back to* SARAH) And that's your best friend speaking! A frank and fearless independent view! You've just go to stop going on and on and on and on and on and on——

(*One by one the participants in the argument have finished. Only* DAVID *continues.*)

—and on and on and on and on and on and on——

(*The other three have turned and are looking at him. Becoming aware that he is the only one speaking he tails off.*)

—and on. (*Pause.*) And on. Yes. Well, what we've got to decide is, are we civilised people or not?

STUART We try to be.

DAVID Good. Then we sit down quietly. With a drink. And we talk this whole thing out.

STUART Like reasonable people.

VALERIE And quietly.

SARAH In a civilised way.

(*During the above* VALERIE *and* SARAH *have sat on one side of the room and* STUART *on the other.* DAVID *has gone into the bedroom and he now returns with a bottle of Portuguese Champagne, bearing a hideous green label, and four glasses. He hands the glasses out and proceeds to open the bottle. He glances ceiling-wards waiting for the cork to shoot out; instead it plops pathetically to the floor. Simultaneously,* SARAH, VALERIE *and* STUART *put aside their glasses.* DAVID *pours himself a glass of Portuguese Champagne and drinks; although it tastes ghastly he tries to look as if he is enjoying it.*)

DAVID Well, I——

(*And at this point the telephone rings. Puzzled, they look at each other.*)

VALERIE (*mystified*) But we're all here.

DAVID (*to* SARAH) Well, answer it!

SARAH You answer it! It's your phone.

DAVID I only pay the bill! (*However he crosses and picks up the telephone.*) David Lord speaking. (*He grimaces in surprise at the rudeness of the person who is ringing up. To* SARAH.) It's for you.

SARAH (*taking the telephone*) Sarah Lord speaking. (*As she listens for quite some considerable time her expression changes to one of disgust and horror.*) I seriously think you need medical attention. (*Pause.*) Well, if that's the kind of language you use, I'm not surprised that he left you. (*She slams down the receiver. To* STUART.) That was your wife.

STUART (*sarcastically*) Oh, thank you very much. Any messages?

SARAH She didn't want to talk to you. She wanted to talk to me.

VALERIE You mean she wanted to talk to me?

SARAH Mmmm. Do you know what she wants to do to you? She wants to take a pair of rusty scissors and——

STUART Do you mind, madam? I will thank you not to bandy my wife's private conversations in public?

SARAH (*sharply*) I'm very sorry, but if your wife is in the habit of making obscene phone calls you can't be surprised that she gets herself talked about.

STUART My wife does not make obscene phone calls.

SARAH She just made one. I got it.

STUART Perhaps so, under extreme pressure. But it is not a habit. (*The telephone rings again and* SARAH *looks queryingly at* STUART.)

SARAH Isn't it?

(STUART *crosses and answers the telephone.*)

STUART Now look here—— (*But he can get no further. He listens for quite some time and his expression, too, changes to one of incredulity and disgust.*) Yes. Quite. Well, luckily for you this doesn't happen to be my telephone. If it were I should report you to the Postmaster General in the public interest. (*He puts down the receiver.*)

SARAH What did she suggest this time?

STUART Many things. (*To* DAVID.) However, it was not my wife. In point of fact, it was for you. A Miss Semolina Silkpaws.

SARAH (*wheeling on* DAVID) Semolina Silkpaws?

VALERIE Meet Squirrel Nutkin.

DAVID That was confidential, madam! (*To* STUART.) What did she say?

(*During the following,* SARAH *marches to the telephone and dials the operator.*)

STUART Apparently the little animal takes issue with you over some telegram or other. She thinks you might benefit from a small surgical operation which she offers to perform herself. (*With a smile at* SARAH.) With a pair of blunt rusty scissors.

DAVID You're a liar!

STUART (*taking offence*) Watch it, old chap!

(STUART *and* DAVID *glare at each other as* SARAH *speaks into the telephone.*)

SARAH Hello, operator. I want to report an obscene telephone call.

DAVID Give me that damn phone!

(*He grabs the telephone from her with such violence that the cord parts company with the set. He bangs down the telephone in disgust.*)

SARAH Now look what you've done!

DAVID Maxine has never uttered the mildest obscenity in all her life.

STUART The girl works in a garage, man! Don't be a complete fool. If she was a decent girl she'd have got a job at Harrods.

DAVID Now listen, dear friend, any more of that and I shall punch your bloody nose! If it comes to being a complete fool, at least I wasn't strung along for three whole months by some woman pretending to be married!

VALERIE (*to* DAVID) I'm not some woman and I didn't string him along!

STUART (*to* VALERIE) You were stringing me along! What else do you call it?

SARAH (*to* STUART) Oh, stop whining! It's cost you nothing! You weren't forking out for posh lunches every day of the week.

DAVID (*to* SARAH) What would you rather I'd done? Put her in the family way?

SARAH Oh, go and hoard your acorns, Squirrel Nutkin.

(STUART *sniggers.*)

DAVID Very well, Sarah. I shall go back to Maxine. There'll be no lunches—food is out. We'll borrow a flat. And I shall go to bed with her at every conceivable opportunity.

SARAH You can do what you like, David. Valerie, you can have this flat every night of the week. Because I shan't be in it.

DAVID (*sneering*) More adultery by proxy?

SARAH By practice. I've had seven years of being married and it's *boring*! I'm going to find a lover, a good, solid dependable married man. I shall tell him I'm a single girl. He'll fall in love with me. It'll be difficult, impracticable, almost impossible—but it will be exciting.

STUART Exciting for who?

SARAH (*exultantly*) Me!

STUART (*bitterly*) Yes. I've been through that—it isn't worth it. Shouting, bawling, lying, quarrelling—you can get all that at home. What a man wants in his life is a little area of peace. Quiet lunches, holding hands in taxis. Probably rather a young girl. Innocent. Yes. I shall go back to my wife and then I shall look elsewhere for affection—but only affection.

(*During the above,* DAVID *has been tinkering with the telephone, trying to poke the cord back into it.*)

DAVID This bloody thing's had it.

VALERIE (*abruptly*) I'm going to get married.

(*They all look at her.*)

I'm sick of the toil and trouble and effort of trying to be a mistress. I shall marry the first man I meet and make his life hell for him.

DAVID (*finally putting down the telephone*) Well, I'll have to ring her from the pub, that's all.

STUART I must ring my wife.

SARAH I'll ring Monica.

VALERIE I shall ring a marriage bureau.

They all look at each other, almost challengingly. Then DAVID *makes a dash for the door. The others rush after him in hot pursuit.*

There is a moment's pause before a mild-looking STRANGER

wanders on past "The Hussar" and enters the telephone box.

DAVID *charges down the stairs and rushes across to the telephone box. The lift doors are flung open and* STUART *and* SARAH *bundle out and also run across to the telephone box.* VALERIE, *carrying her shoes in order to run faster, patters down the stairs and also scampers across to the telephone box. Ignoring each other completely, the four of them form an orderly queue.*

CURTAIN

PROPERTY LIST

ACT ONE

The Flat
  Front door shut
  Bedroom door open
  Lift blind up

Desk U.C.
  On it:
    Telephone
    Table lamp
    Ashtray
    Letters

  In L. *drawer*
    Two telephone directories, with A-D volume on top

  In C. *drawer*
    Various letters etc.

  Under desk
    Wastepaper basket

Drinks table L.C.
  On top:
    Seven whisky glasses
    Open bottle of gin (top on but lifted)
    Empty whisky bottle
    Brandy bottle
    Martini bottle
    Jug of water
    Soda syphon (half-full)
    Full tonic bottle

Half-full tonic bottle
Large bottle opener
Spare bottle opener
Ashtray
DAVID's hat

On shelf
Six small soda bottles
Three dry ginger bottles
Full whisky bottle D.S. end with top free for quick opening

Small table D.L.
On it:
Ashtray with lipstick-covered cigarette butt set out of view of audience
Cigarette box containing three cigars and two cigarettes
Cigarette lighter (practical)

Sofa table behind sofa
On it:
Photograph of SARAH in standing frame
Large ashtray

Chest D.R.
On it:
'Evening Standard' open at Entertainments page
Three glossy magazines
Suede shoe brush

Phone box
On top shelf
Two spare threepenny pieces

Bottom shelf
London telephone directories, with E-K placed sideways on top of others

Offstage
U.R. ("Hussar")
Pint tankard (DAVID)
Glass of whisky (DAVID)
Two cigars (DAVID)

Spare glass of water (DAVID)
Three glasses of whisky (SARAH)
Two glasses of gin (STUART)
One glass of gin (VALERIE)
Bottle of Beaujolais (DAVID)

U.L. (Bedroom)
Two identical housecoats (VALERIE and SARAH)
Two pairs of matching shoes (VALERIE and SARAH)
Two pairs of scissors (VALERIE and SARAH)
Suitcase with initials S.L. (SARAH)
Jacket with note in top breast pocket (SARAH)
Pair of trousers with leg cut off (DAVID)
Seven bottles of toiletries (DAVID)
Spare ashtray (for offstage use by DAVID)

D.R.
Suitcase (STUART)
In it:
Pyjamas on top
Razor, toothbrush, etc.
Towel with large 'HIS' printed on it

Umbrella (STUART)

ACT TWO

The Flat
Front door shut
Bedroom door shut
Lift blind down

Strike
Practical lighter from small table
Full soda syphon
Dirty glasses
One tonic water
Scissors
Cut sleeves

SET:

Non-practical lighter on small table
Empty soda syphon on drinks table
Four clean whisky glasses on drinks table
Maxine's note under ashtray on sofa table
DAVID's tankard and bottle of Beaujolais in phone box
Large bottle opener on hook on D.S. side of drinks table
Half-opened cellophane cover on cigar in cigarette box
SARAH's photograph on sofa table
Open Cologne bottle on sofa table

Offstage

U.L. (Bedroom)

Bottle of Portuguese Champagne
Four champagne glasses

PERSONAL

DAVID Watch
Wallet
Handkerchief
Three threepenny pieces
Keys

SARAH Handbag containing purse, mirror, lipstick
Watch
One threepenny piece
Keys

STUART Cigarette case with five cigarettes
Lighter
Wallet with seven pound notes and dummy spares
Four threepenny pieces
Three pennies
Handkerchief
Spectacles

VALERIE Handbag containing framed photograph of herself, to match SARAH's photograph on stage, and handkerchief
Key ring
Cigarette case with two cigarettes
Lighter
Three threepenny pieces

SOUND EFFECTS

A recording of the telephone pips and of the lift rising and descending can be obtained from Bishop Sound and Electrical Co. Ltd., 48 Monmouth Street, London, W.C.2.

THE LIFT

In the original production there was a Perspex window above the lift door, so that the lift could be seen rising and descending. This effect is obtained by the following method. A light inside the lift is left on all the time. A blind is fixed behind and below the window and is drawn up as the lift rises, and lowered as the lift comes down. In other words, all that is seen is the light, which appears to vanish upwards and reappear coming down. The sound must be synchronised with this.

The back 'wall' of the lift must, of course, be a door, so that the actors can pass through.

STAGE PLAN

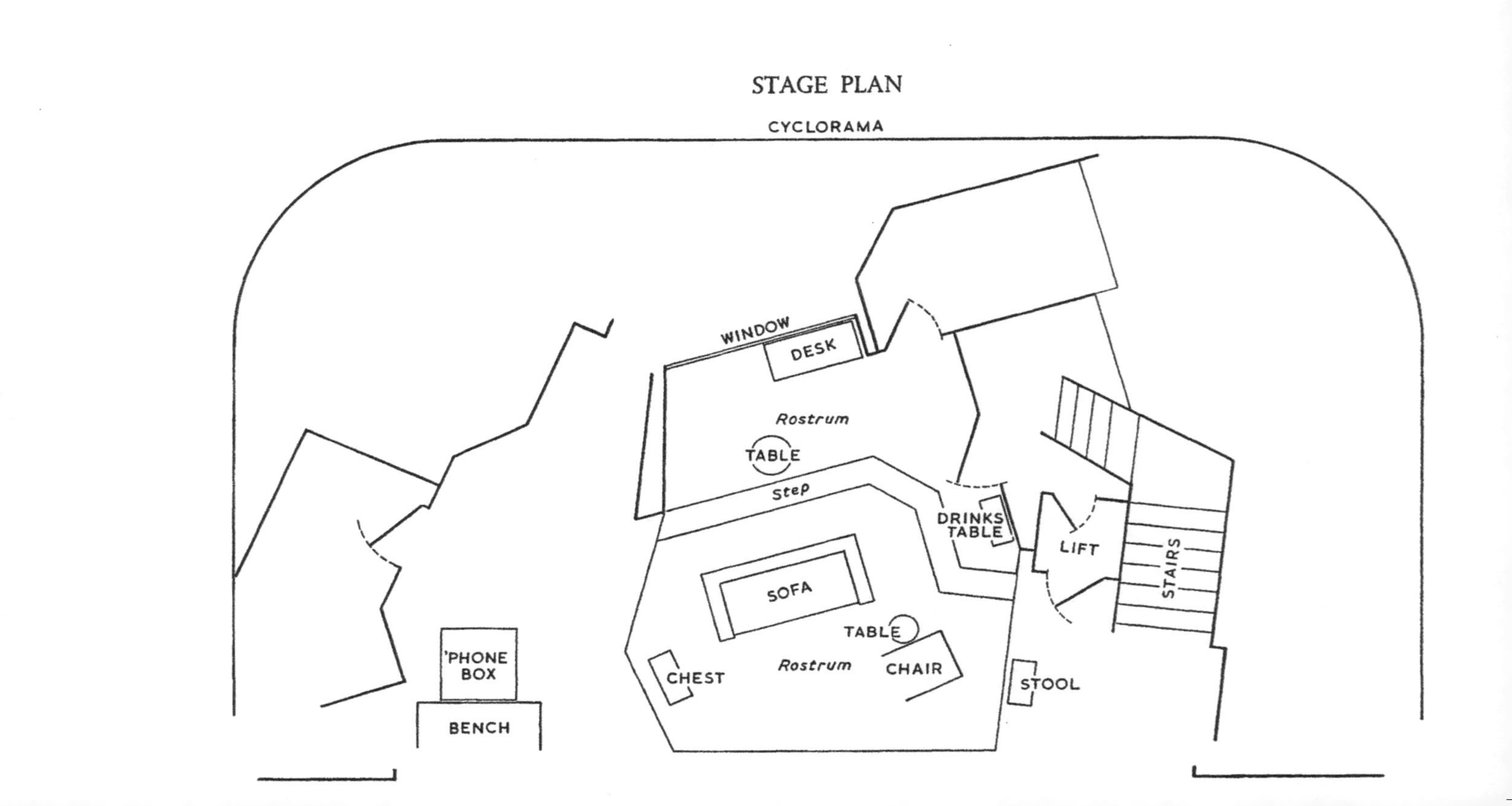
CYCLORAMA
WINDOW
DESK
Rostrum
TABLE
Step
DRINKS TABLE
LIFT
STAIRS
SOFA
TABLE
CHAIR
CHEST
Rostrum
STOOL
'PHONE BOX
BENCH

SOME PRESS OPINIONS OF THIS PLAY

Say Who You Are may not be absolutely the best play in London, but it is certainly the funniest. It is socially adventurous, too, which is rare for a farce. This may even produce misgivings among neo-reactionaries, who would limit criticism and ridicule to fashionable targets; for *Say Who You Are*, whilst milking such universally acceptable scapegoats as social climbers, sun-trap villas in Spain, and habitués of the Caprice and the Mirabelle, is also riotously amusing at the expense of semi-sacred objects like French films (or plays, for that matter), and the working classes. But for anyone who can take a joke without shouting for mercy this play offers the most carefree, the most recklessly happy evening to be spent anywhere in London. It is a recipe for undiluted joy, and I laughed until my eyes were blinded with tears.—Harold Hobson, *Sunday Times*

It looks as if Her Majesty's Theatre has a box office success on its hands. Last night's new comedy *Say Who You Are* is one of those loud, low, cheerful, married mix-ups which delight the casual theatre-goer in search of brassy vulgar entertainment.—Philip Hope-Wallace, *The Guardian*

This is a clever and funny farce by two experts at the genre.—Peter Lewis, *Daily Mail*

Say Who You Are is the kind of play which years ago used to be rather too common in the West End theatre. Now it has rarity value, which ensures it a welcome. A bright, brittle near-farce, by those practised artificers, Keith Waterhouse and Willis Hall, it is aimed to hit the popular taste and seems likely to land bang in the middle of the target . . . Good unclean fun.—W. A. Darlington, *Daily Telegraph*

That never-ending battle—the war of independence between husband and wife, is the main theme of *Say Who You Are*. The verbal skirmishes are frequently very funny and had the audience rocking, especially in the second act. The four characters weave in and out of bedroom and bar at a rare pace in some cleverly contrived situations. —Arthur Thirkell, *Daily Mirror*

Lightning Source UK Ltd.
Milton Keynes UK
UKOW06f0412050816

280024UK00001B/65/P